In the Morning When I Rise

REFLECTIONS TO CENTER YOUR DAY ON HIM

Kim Vogel Sawyer

In the Morning When I Rise

REFLECTIONS TO CENTER YOUR DAY ON HIM

Kim Vogel Sawyer

WITH PHOTOGRAPHY BY PHOEBE JANZEN

© 2019 Kim Vogel Sawyer

Published by Wings of Hope Publishing Group
Established 2013
www.wingsofhopepublishing.com
Find us on Facebook: Search "Wings of Hope"

Printed in the United States of America.

All rights reserved. No part of this publication may be reproduced, stored in a retrieval system, or transmitted in any form or by any means—for example, electronic, photocopy, recording—without the prior written permission of the publisher. The only exception is brief quotations in printed reviews.

Sawyer, Kim Vogel
    In the Morning When I Rise / Kim Vogel Sawyer
    Wings of Hope Publishing Group
    ISBN: 978-1-944309-38-1
    ISBN: 978-1-944309-39-8 (eBook)

All scripture taken from the King James Version, a public domain text in the United States.

Cover design and typesetting by Vogel Design LLC in Wichita, Kansas. Photography for devotionals provided by Phoebe Janzen.

INTRODUCTION

*The Lord looked down from heaven upon the children of men,
to see if there were any that did understand, and seek God.*
PSALM 14:2

A friend of mine, a relatively new Christian, called me one morning and told me she'd found a way to make her whole day go better—"I start out reading from the Bible and talking to God." She'd discovered, as so many Christians before her, that focusing on Him first helped her stay focused on Him as the day progressed.

Life is busy and hectic and distracting. It tries to gobble up our time and rob of us intimate minutes with the Father. But God is always on alert, always searching for a fragile, wilting soul who pauses in the stress and strain of life and looks upward. In that moment, He reaches down and draws us close. That's how much He wants fellowship with us. Are you feeling parched and lonely? Look up, meet His gaze, and find your blessed refreshment.

Kim Vogel Sawyer

> Therefore if any man be in Christ,
> he is a new creature:
> old things are passed away;
> behold, all things are become new.
> —2 Corinthians 5:15

JANUARY 1

What better message for the first day of a new year than a reminder of the new life that comes through faith in Christ? The old is gone, the new is come thanks to redemption's story. No more darkness abides in my soul, because I've been flooded with the light of Christ's mercy.

Is there someone on your prayer list who is still lost in sin's abyss? Let's pray together that this is the year your dear one will find salvation and be transferred into the Light of life.

---

*Heavenly Father, thank You for loving us enough to send Your Son.
I lift my lost loved one to You today and ask You
to work Your perfect will in bringing salvation.*

He hath made his wonderful works to be remembered: the Lord is gracious and full of compassion.
—Psalm 111:4

JANUARY 2

I love God's Word. Every time I read it, I find familiar scripture and stories and people who inspire me. Every time I read it, I find something new that I can apply to my life. He gave us His Word so we can remember what He's done, remember what He's promised, remember what He expects from His children. He is gracious and compassionate and wishes every person ever born to know Him. Do you want to find Him? Open His Word...He will meet your need.

Heavenly Father, thank You for the Bible,
Your inspired words of instruction and affirmation.
May I absorb Your words and live them
so others can see the difference they make.

Fear not: for I have redeemed thee, I have called thee by thy name; thou art mine. When thou passest through the waters, I will be with thee; and through the rivers, they shall not overflow thee: when thou walkest through the fire, thou shalt not be burned; neither shall the flame kindle upon thee. For I am the Lord thy God, the Holy One of Israel, thy Saviour...
—Isaiah 43:2-3

JANUARY 3

Several years ago I had a sad conversation with one of my grandchildren, who said very somberly, "Gramma, sometimes this world scares me." I know what was meant. Lots of scary things—such as terrorist attacks, major storms, or evil actions—happen, and we don't have control over any of it. Back during a dark, scary, uncertain time in my life I clung to these verses from Isaiah and claimed them as my promise from God: no matter what I face, He will be with me, because I am His and He is mine. There are very few sureties in life (besides "death and taxes," my mother used to say), but I know without even a smidgen of doubt, the Holy One of Israel, my Savior, is with me through the waters, the rivers, and the fires. Resting in that truth eases my fear.

---

*Heavenly Father, thank You for never leaving me
to face the floods or fires of life alone.
Thank You for being my Savior.*

*Return unto thy rest, O my soul;
for the Lord hath dealt bountifully
with thee.*
—Psalm 116:7

JANUARY 4

I've had the privilege of walking with the Lord for more than five decades. I asked Jesus to be my Savior when I was eight years old. Over the years, the Lord has proven His ability to be my Strength, Comforter, Advisor, and ever-present Friend. In moments when melancholy or sorrow strikes, I know I can rest in His arms and find a place of peace. My soul always has a reason to rejoice, regardless of circumstances, because the Lord has been good to me.

---

*Heavenly Father, I rejoice in my salvation.
I rejoice in the knowledge of Your love for me.
I rejoice because You are good.
Thank You for the blessed gift of rest.*

*Ye are my witnesses, saith the Lord,
and my servant whom I have chosen:
that ye may know and believe me,
and understand that I am he:
before me there was no God formed,
neither shall there be after me.
I, even I, am the Lord;
and beside me there is no saviour.*
—Isaiah 43:10-11

JANUARY 5

There are lots of people who believe there is no God. Then there are some who say, "Sure, I believe in God," but their lives don't reflect a holy reverence for the LORD. Still more say, "God is love, so everybody gets to Him one way or another." These kinds of comments make my heart ache, because these people—while very sincere—are very lost. God is God is God, who was and is and will always be. He sent Jesus into the world to be our Savior, the Rescuer from sin's claim on our souls. Obviously God loves us or He wouldn't have sent Jesus, but we have a responsibility to accept Jesus. Until we do, all we have is a head knowledge—our heart is still cold and stained from sin. Those of us who know the truth, who've been cleansed and changed thanks to the precious Blood of Jesus, must be witnesses to His presence. This messed up world desperately needs the Savior.

*Heavenly Father, thank You for revealing Yourself to me
and bringing me to saving grace.
May I be a witness to the truth of who You are.*

Remember ye not the former things, neither consider the things of old. Behold, I will do a new thing; now it shall spring forth; shall ye not know it? I will even make a way in the wilderness, and rivers in the desert.
—Isaiah 43:18-19

JANUARY 6

Oh, how the ol' devil likes to remind us of our past mistakes and failures. You see, if he can keep us down and defeated, he can interfere with our fellowship with God and keep us from living a triumphant life. God is about making things new. Not made over. Not patched up and recycled. *Made new.* Yes, we need to learn from our past mistakes, but wallowing in failure does us no good.

Christian brother or sister, if regret is weighing you down, read today's verses again and thank the Lord for the new way He is carving for you—no longer bound by sins' chains but free to run headlong on the path of grace. Hallelujah!

Heavenly Father, I praise You for the power of forgiveness and the new life You've given me in Your Son. Thank You for my freedom! May my life reflect my gratitude in all I do and say.

> *I, even I, am he
> that blotteth out thy
> transgressions
> for mine own sake,
> and will not remember thy sins.*
> —Isaiah 43:25

JANUARY 7

As far as the east is from the west, God has removed the penalty of sin from those who call on Him with a sincere desire to make Him Lord of their lives. Sometimes when I look in the mirror, I do a double-take. What is that woman with crow's feet, gray hair, and sagging jowls doing standing in front of me? Other days I look at my reflection and sorrow over the hurtful things I've said or done, and I have a hard time meeting my own gaze. But God—our infinitely loving and forgiving God—sees something else when He looks at me. Because I've asked forgiveness for my sins, God doesn't see even one of them. They're gone. Thus, He sees His child, His beloved, His holy one. He has blotted out those things that separated me from Him and remembers them no more. That truth makes me weep with joy and humility.

---

*Thank You, dear Father, for Your unfailing and unfathomable love.
Let me walk worthy of You.*

> For I know the thoughts that I think toward you, saith the Lord, thoughts of peace, and not of evil, to give you an expected end.
> —Jeremiah 29:11

JANUARY 8

Can we get personal? The Bible was written a long time ago, but its words are still applicable to each of us today. So look at the scripture and consider: God is speaking to you. He loves you enough to make good plans for your life, plans that will bring you joy and fulfillment. Those plans start with your acceptance of Jesus Christ as your Savior and Lord. When we become His, then His plans can be set in motion. Have you accepted the gift of salvation and asked Jesus to take the reins of your life? If not, why not do so today? A life of joy, peace, and contentment is waiting.

Heavenly Father, thank You for the plans You've made for my life, plans intended to bring me joy and give You glory. May I never doubt my salvation and the love You have for me.

> Now as he walked by the sea of Galilee,
> he saw Simon and Andrew his brother
> casting a net into the sea:
> for they were fishers.
> —Mark 1:16

JANUARY 9

J love the hidden meaning in this simple statement. Jesus saw Simon and Andrew. Fishermen. Rough men. Smelly and dirty. But when He looked at them, He *saw* what they could be. When Jesus looks at you, He *sees* what you can be. He sees your heart, your deepest desires, your potential, and He *knows* what will bring you joy. Jesus doesn't see as the world sees. He sees the best you He knows you can be. Why then, would we trust anyone else with our lives?

Heavenly Father, thank You for seeing me
with eyes of grace, love, and mercy.
Help me achieve the potential You see in me
so I might bring You glory and honor.

...Christ in you, the hope of glory.
—Colossians 1:27b

JANUARY 10

God makes wonderful plans for His children. He sees potential in each of us, He offers His guidance for us to achieve our potential, and He gives us what we need to help us weather the storms of life. Why does He invests so much of Himself in us? It's simple: so we might reflect Him to others. Your words, actions, and attitudes can impact those you encounter. When you love as God loves, when you stand strong against adversity, when you are calm despite the raging seas, you show others the difference Christ makes in a person's life. You become God's messenger.

Being His reflection is an awesome privilege and responsibility. And one day, when you stand before Him, He will point to those who came to know Him because of your witness. What a joyful day that will be!

Heavenly Father, thank You for giving me the Spirit of Your Son. May my every word and deed be a witness to the hope I possess because of Your Son's sacrifice at Calvary.

Now set your heart and your soul to seek the Lord your God...
—1 Chronicles 22:19a

JANUARY 11

Have you ever been torn and uncertain? Life is fraught with decisions—some little, some big—that bring consequences. Sometimes we become so bogged down with worry we find ourselves frozen in place instead of moving forward. Here's our motion-jogger: *seek the Lord*. When we seek Him and His will above everything else, His Spirit whispers direction. We move forward with confidence, believing that whatever we face, He will be with us and will strengthen us. If you're trapped in a season of uncertainty, look to Him. He will be your Guide.

---

*Heavenly Father, open my eyes to seek You first and fully.
Let my steps remains on Your pathway.
Give me the confidence to do Your will.*

...he that cometh to God must believe that he is, and that he is a rewarder of them that diligently seek him.
—Hebrews 11:6b

JANUARY 12

I took my middle daughter's boys to the grocery store with me when they were about seven and eight years old. They asked, "Gramma, if we're good, can we have quarters for the vending machines?" I said, "How about being good just because it will make Gramma happy?" After a moment's consideration, they agreed that was reward enough.

God rewards us when we truly seek to honor Him. He rewards us with His presence, His comfort, His peace and strength. He rewards us by preparing a place for us in Heaven. His rewards can't be measured by human standards, and they are greater than anything this world can offer. For a satisfying, joy-filled life, seek Him. The return on your investment is immeasurable!

Heavenly Father, thank You for Your promise of eternity. May Your presence now and in the time to come be all the reward I need.

*My soul, wait thou only upon God;
for my expectation is from him.*
—Psalm 62:5

JANUARY 13

Hope is one of my favorite words. Holding onto hope brings peace in the most troubling times. Hardships and trials can rob us of hope in what really matters if we allow worry to consume us. We cannot place hope for our future in anything this world offers—our hope must rest in God alone, for He alone can save us for eternity. When temptation to wallow in despair attacks you, close your eyes, speak the name of His Son...Jesus...and remind yourself that He is our only Hope and Stay. Peace will descend in your soul.

---

*Heavenly Father, thank You for Your presence.
Let me rest in You and You alone,
growing in trust and faith.*

And ye shall seek me, and find me, when ye shall search for me with all your heart.
—Jeremiah 29:13

JANUARY 14

Most of us are familiar with Jeremiah 29:11, the scripture that reminds us God makes good plans for His children. In verse 13, we find the reminder of how to uncover His plans: seek Him with all your heart. The heart is the center of our being, where our values and deepest beliefs are found. When we turn our heart to Him and seek Him above all else, then the pathway to goodness, mercy, and blessings opens before us. He's waiting, arms wide, for us to run toward Him. We find Him when we seek Him with our whole heart.

---

*Heavenly Father, You are always available to any who seek You.
Let my eyes remain on You,
and may my heart always seek to honor You.*

And being in an agony he prayed more earnestly; and his sweat was as it were great drops of blood falling down to the ground.
—Luke 22:44

JANUARY 15

Jesus knew what pain and agony He would suffer in order to do His Father's will, and the deep anguish He poured out in prayer resulted in sweat drops of blood. Many times I've been anguished and prayed with a heavy, burdened heart. I've never dripped blood in place of sweat, but there have been times my sorrow was so great no words would form. In those times, when my prayers turn to wordless groanings, Jesus Himself interprets them for the Father. Having been human, Jesus understands my human emotions. Being able to trust Him to hear, care, and answer my prayers brings hope even in the midst of heartache. I am so grateful He is always there for me!

Heavenly Father, thank You for the interceder, Jesus Christ, who speaks for me when I am burdened and wordless. Please hear and respond to the groaning of my aching heart. I trust You to answer in the way that is best for me.

> But Jesus called them unto him and said, Suffer the little children to come unto me, and forbid them not: for of such is the kingdom of God.
> —Luke 18:16

JANUARY 16

Jesus didn't mean that only those the age of children would make up the kingdom of God; He meant that those who came must exhibit a childlike trust. Babies arrive unable to meet their own needs. When they cry, they trust that someone will satisfy their hunger or ease their discomfort or assure them they aren't alone. The older we get, the harder it can be to trust, because we've experienced situations where people proved untrustworthy. But Jesus is completely trustworthy. He keeps His promises. We don't need to hold back in fear or apprehension. We can place ourselves in His keeping and know that our every need will be met. He already knows all about us and He loves us anyway, so we can trust Him with our very hearts and souls.

Heavenly Father, please erase any fears or insecurities
from my heart and let me trust You fully.
Let me experience the freedom
complete surrender to You provides.

> *Since we heard of your faith in Christ Jesus, and of the love which ye have to all the saints, For the hope which is laid up for you in heaven...*
> —Colossians 1:4-5a

JANUARY 17

People try to place their hope in the stock market, or in a new boyfriend/girlfriend, or in a bigger house with lots of rooms. But the only hope that endures is the promise waiting for us in heaven. Does it not brings us joy when we know those we love also have mansions reserved in heaven where we will reside with our Savior eternally? Speak loudly of your faith. Spread the truth of what you've learned: Jesus is hope's Anchor. Keep sharing until everyone you know has heard the message of salvation. They need the Good News.

Heavenly Father, thank You for the hope You've given me.
Embolden me to share my faith
so that others will come to know the hope of heaven.

> The Lord is my strength and song,
> and he is become my salvation:
> he is my God, and I will prepare him
> an habitation; my father's God,
> and I will exalt him.
> —Exodus 15:2

JANUARY 18

When my heart is heavy or I'm battling pain—emotional, spiritual, or physical—I've learned a simple pick-me-up: I sing praise songs. One after another.

You see, God inhabits praise, so when I lift my voice in praise and adoration, He infuses me. When He infuses me, I discover the strength I need to face the conflict. Exodus 15:2 sounds simplistic, but it's so true. He *is* my strength and my song.

Heavenly Father, remind me that no circumstance can ever change
who You are to me or who I am to You.
Let me raise a voice of praise and exaltation to You,
my Strength and Song.

> Seek the Lord and his strength,
> seek his face continually.
> —1 Chronicles 16:11

JANUARY 19

Have you ever spent time observing someone you admired? Even without intending to do so, we begin to emulate that person, taking on some of their mannerisms and behaviors. This is exactly what God wants us to do with Him. When we seek Him, we find Him; when we ask for His strength, He grants it. The more we seek His face, the more we reflect Him. So make your search constant—a search to deepen and expand and solidify your relationship with Him.

Heavenly Father, thank You for being the example I can always follow.
Thank You for always leading me on the correct path.
Draw my eyes and heart to You above anyone or anything else.

> *Remember his marvelous works that he hath done, his wonders, and the judgments of his mouth.*
> —1 Chronicles 16:12

JANUARY 20

God's incredible ability to forgive never ceases to astound me. No matter how far from His pathways we've roamed, no matter how lost we might feel, a heartfelt word of confession brings a rush of grace that washes away the stains and brings us into right relationship with Him again. He is so faithful. His justice is always fair and right. What an amazing Father-God we have...

Heavenly Father, thank You for Your willingness to forgive every wrong.
Thank You for wanting a relationship with me.
May I grow to want You more and more.

*Who comforteth us in all our tribulation,
that we may be able to comfort them
which are in any trouble,
by the comfort wherewith we ourselves
are comforted of God.*
—2 Corinthians 1:4

JANUARY 21

If you've walked with the Lord for any length of time, I'm sure you can recall a time when you experienced the warmth and presence of His comforting touch. But you know, He doesn't only comfort us to help us; He comforts us to give us an example of how to comfort others. No hardship, no heartache, no failure is wasted in God's kingdom. We can reach out and offer hope and help to others facing similar situations. Comfort others in the way that you've been comforted by God—you can be His hands right here on earth.

*Heavenly Father, thank You for comforting me
in times of heartache and despair.
May my heart be open to offering Your love
to hurting souls I encounter.*

> *For I am not ashamed of the gospel of Christ: for it is the power of God unto salvation to every one that believeth; to the Jew first, and also to the Greek.*
> —Romans 1:16

JANUARY 22

Salvation is a glorious gift, undeserved yet offered willingly and lovingly. God surrendered His precious Son for us; Jesus died a horrendous, painful, humiliating death for our sins. So often when we speak of our Father and Savior, the world claims to be "offended," and then—far too frequently—we hush rather than be branded intolerant or narrow-minded. But here's the thing...when we cease to share the gospel, we are denying the One who saved us. When we hush, we hide the truth from those who desperately need to hear it. We cannot be ashamed of the gospel. We must proclaim the way to salvation. because too many are marching in the wrong direction.

---

*Heavenly Father, thank You for sending Your Son
to take the penalty for my sins.
Please embolden me to proclaim His name openly and unashamedly
until everyone knows that Jesus Christ is Lord!*

> *That if thou shall confess with thy mouth the Lord Jesus, and shalt believe in thine heart that God hath raised him from the dead, thou shalt be saved.*
> —Romans 10:9

JANUARY 23

One of the things I love most about Christianity is its simplicity. Believe, confess it aloud, and you are saved. No dues to pay, no deeds to perform, no rules to follow. Simply believe. When we accept Jesus, the Holy Spirit indwells us, providing us with a constant Companion and Guide who helps us grow Christlike in our actions and attitudes. You see, Christianity isn't a religion, but a way of life—a way that lasts eternally.

Heavenly Father, thank You for providing a way to reach You.
Thank You for the gift of my salvation.
Thank You that I needn't worry about endless rituals or rules but simply walk in Your grace.

> *For whosoever shall call upon the name of the Lord shall be saved.*
> —Romans 10:13

JANUARY 24

One of the most heartbreaking things I've ever heard anyone say is "God wouldn't want me." It's heartbreaking because the speaker believes it's true, but I know differently. God didn't send Jesus for a select few; God sent Jesus to save every soul that has ever been born and will ever be born. But He doesn't force us to follow Him; He waits for us to willingly receive His Son. Everyone—the vilest sinner, the most tender spirit, whether old, young, rich, or poor—is offered the same gift of salvation. One only needs to accept it. Call upon the name of the Lord and you *will* be saved.

---

*Heavenly Father, thank You for not waiting for me
to be "good enough" for You, but receiving me as I am—
needy and flawed and broken.
Thank You for loving me enough to heal my sinful soul
so I may stand holy and righteous before You.*

And to know the love of Christ, which passeth knowledge, that ye might be filled with all the fulness of God.
—Ephesians 3:19

JANUARY 25

When I was a little girl, I puzzled over the concept that God's love for me had been, currently was, and would be forever. Everything else had a beginning and end. Not until I was expecting my first child did I find a small similarity: even before my daughter was born, I already loved her. If she were to leave me through death or abandonment, I would still love her. My love for her would last for as long as I lasted.

My love for my child is not as vast as God's love for us, but I've come to believe He loved me before I came to be and that His love will always be with me (see Psalm 139). We might not be able to fully comprehend everything about God, but that doesn't need to keep us from accepting the truth that He loves us unconditionally and without time constraints. His love for us is the only certainty in this world.

---

*Heavenly Father, thank You for loving me.
Grow me more deeply in faith
so I know the fullness of Your presence.*

> But the manifestation of the Spirit is given to every man to profit withal.
> —1 Corinthians 12:7

JANUARY 26

I appreciate having the Holy Spirit as my Guide, my Strength-giver, my Comfort-bringer, my Companion. But those are all "for me" reasons. There's a deeper reason why God gives an indwelling of the Holy Spirit—for others' good. If we rely on the Holy Spirit's guidance, we're less likely to say or do hurtful things in a moment of frustration or anger. If we listen to His voice and heed it, we will be a better example of Jesus to those around us. Reflecting Him is always best for the Body of Christ and for the world in general.

Heavenly Father, thank You for the indwelling of Your Spirit. Before I speak or react, let me seek You first so I do good rather than harm to those You love.

> Now ye are the body of Christ, and members in particular.
> —1 Corinthians 12:27

JANUARY 27

I was such a bashful kid—rarely smiled or talked, always nervous that somebody might notice me. I remain a first-class introvert. The problem with shyness is the feeling that you don't belong. But praise God, when it comes to being part of the body of Christ, all one needs is faith. I don't have to be lonely because I am never alone. I don't have to feel left out because I am His.

There's no better "club" than being a member of the body of Christ, because it comes with an eternal membership.

---

*Heavenly Father, thank You
for making me a part of the body of Christ.
May I contribute in a positive manner
and be a benefit to Your Kingdom.*

God hath tempered the body together, having given more abundant honor to that part which lacked. That there should be no schism in the body; but that the members should have the same care one for another. And whether one member suffer, all the members suffer with it; or one member be honoured, all the members rejoice with it.
—I Corinthians 12:24b-26

JANUARY 28

I love how God designed the Body of Christ. Every member has a purpose that benefits the body as a whole. His desire is for us to encourage and support one other, to mourn with those who mourn and rejoice with those who rejoice. Our unity shows those looking on that we love one other. Our love draws them in and they discover the love of Christ for themselves. That line in a song from my teen years, "They will know we are Christians by our love," is very true.

Heavenly Father, it is a privilege and honor to be part of Your family.
May I behave in a way that brings glory to the whole,
and may I never create strife.
Let me be honorable in my dealings with fellow believers
and an example of Your grace to all who I encounter.

> Unto thee I will cry,
> O Lord my rock;
> —Psalm 28:1a

JANUARY 29

When I was a little girl, one of my favorite "Sunday School" songs was about the foolish man and the wise man. One man built his house on sand, the other on a rock, and when storms came the house built on sand collapsed while the one built on the rock stood firm. The final verse said, "So build your house on the Lord Jesus Christ…"

As Christians, we never have to "hang in there"—we can stand firm on the foundation of Jesus. So when trouble strikes, when grief ascends, when worry nips at your heels, call on the Lord. He is the strength you need to weather any storm.

---

*Heavenly Father, You are my Rock and my Stronghold.
Keep my feet planted on Your foundation
and let me stand firmly on Your promises.*

> Blessed be the Lord, because he hath heard the voice of my supplication.
> —Psalm 28:6

JANUARY 30

Have you ever wanted to stand in the middle of a crowded room and yell, "Will someone please listen to me?" That urge struck me now and then when I was growing up because I was the kind of kid people overlooked. (It happens when you're too shy to talk to anyone; eventually they kind of forget you're there.) I spent a lot of time whispering to Jesus in the solitude of my bedroom, and you know, there was a lot of comfort in knowing He always heard me.

If you feel as though no one cares, no one listens, no one truly understands, you're—please take this the right way—wrong. Because He cares deeply. Call on Him. His ears are always tuned to the cries of His children.

Heavenly Father, thank You
that You are always available to hear my cries.
Thank You for caring enough to answer in Your perfect way.
Blessed be Your Name.

...as thy days, so shall thy strength be.
—Deuteronomy 33:25b

JANUARY 31

Let's face it, some days are harder to handle than others. If you've spent the day at a loved one's hospital bedside, or had to lay a dear friend to rest, or received news that impacted your world for every tomorrow, you know what I mean by "harder to handle." My strength has its limits. Praise the Lord, my Father's does not. His strength is immeasurable. And when I need His strength, He is only a prayer away.

Heavenly Father, when I am weak, You are strong.
Surround me with Your strength and give me the courage and ability
to forge forward when times are hard.
To You, Lord, will be given the glory when I stand triumphant.

Seek the Lord and his strength, seek his face continually.
—1 Chronicles 16:11

FEBRUARY 1

Would you like to know the key to indescribable peace, unlimited joy, and abundant contentment? This scripture provides it: Seek *Him*; seek Him *continually*. Before looking to human relationships, money, success, purchases, food, or whatever else our physical shell might reach out to for comfort, seek *Him*. Nothing satisfies like Jesus. He is the Light we need to flood our thirsty, needy soul.

---

*Heavenly Father, thank You for being my Fulfiller.
If there is something in my life that interferes
with my fellowship with You, please make me aware of it
and give me the ability to rid myself of its distraction.*

> *For when we were yet without strength, in due time Christ died for the ungodly.*
> —Romans 5:6

FEBRUARY 2

From the beginning of time, God had a plan to send His Son into the world and offer mankind a way to reach Him and call Him Father. In His perfect timing, God sent Christ, who served as *our* sin sacrifice. Such an enormous sacrifice, such an indescribable gift. It isn't available for purchase. We can't earn it. We can't barter for it. All we have to do is ask, and He forgives our transgressions, gives us a clean slate, and then strengthens us to walk uprightly. The gift of salvation is priceless beyond compare, yet it's available to all who choose to believe.

Heavenly Father, thank You for Your unconditional love for mankind and Your willingness to accept the most shameful among us into Your family.

Then we which are alive and remain shall be caught up together with them in the clouds, to meet the Lord in the air: and so shall we ever be with the Lord.
—1 Thessalonians 4:17

FEBRUARY 3

A marvelous day is coming when Jesus Christ, our risen Lord and Savior, will appear in the clouds. The thought of this event frightened me when I was a kid. I suppose the uncertainty of when it would happen made me nervous. I didn't relish being caught unaware. What if I was in the bathtub? (Yes, childish thinking at its best.) But then when I was in my early twenties, I had a dream that Jesus returned. I felt myself being swept upward. Joy exploded through me, and I awakened reaching for heaven with tears of happiness raining down my cheeks. When I realized I'd only been dreaming, my joy changed to sorrow. From that moment, I've eagerly anticipated Jesus's return.

Maybe I'll see Him when my soul leaves my body in death; maybe I'll see Him on the day of His return. Either way, I will be with Him forever. There is such peace and security in this knowledge.

---

*Heavenly Father, while I wait,
may I live in a way that points others to the One
who will come and claim His own.*

The Lord will give strength unto his people; the Lord will bless his people with peace.
—Psalm 29:11

FEBRUARY 4

Isn't it amazing how, at the height of a tragedy, hope rises? I've seen it so many times in my lifetime—on 9/11, after hurricanes or tornadoes or floods, after mass shootings. Instead of hardship crippling the community, people come together with strength, dignity, and a determination to go on. I believe this ability to stand strong is more than human pride; I believe it is a gift from God. There's no other explanation for peace in the midst of conflict than God bestowing it.

If He can give peace after heartbreaking events, then He can give it to you in the middle of whatever personal trials you are facing. Ask. Trust. He gives peace the world cannot explain nor take away.

Heavenly Father, thank You for peace
that passes all understanding.
May my unexplainable peace prove Your presence
to those who need to see You.

> Great peace have they which love thy law: and nothing shall offend them.
> —Psalm 119:165

FEBRUARY 5

Sometimes events outside of our control bring trouble to our door; other times we race headlong into trouble. When we're in trouble, we aren't very peaceful. So how do we avoid putting ourselves in troubling situations? Very simple: we heed His instructions. When we follow God's guidance, we experience the peace of knowing we are in right standing with our Maker. When we stay on His pathway, we are much less likely to stumble into sin where no peace can be found. Feeling uneasy? Ask God to forgive your errors and then follow His instructions. Peace will descend.

---

*Heavenly Father, thank You for preparing a pathway for me.
Help me stay the course and rest in assurance
that I am in right relationship with You,
for only with You will I discover deep down peace.*

> Christ hath redeemed us from the curse of the law, being made a curse for us: for it is written, Cursed is every one that hangeth on a tree:
> —Galatians 3:13

FEBRUARY 6

First there was the Law. "Do this," "Don't do that," "Avoid this," "Partake of that"... How could anyone keep it all straight? We were destined for failure. Then came redemption. Pardon for sin and a grace that promised to endure. Christ becoming a curse opened the door to endless blessing for us. Praise His name!

Heavenly Father, thank You that in Your great love and compassion
You made a way for us to call You Father.
Thank You, Jesus, for Your sacrifice for me.
I am blessed because of You, and I praise You
for all You give and for all You do for lowly me.

Forasmuch as ye know that ye were not redeemed with corruptible things, as silver and gold, from your vain conversation received by tradition from your fathers;
—1 Peter 1:18

FEBRUARY 7

Redemption is something we often sing about and see as a gift. But how often do we consider the price that was paid for the gift? Christ purchased our redemption through the most painful, humiliating, undeserved death any man could suffer. His willingness to subject Himself to the cross led to our freedom from sin and shame. Will you take a few minutes today and thank Him for the sacrifice He made for you?

Heavenly Father, You sent Your Son to a world that would reject Him. We were undeserving, lost, and rebellious, and still You sent Him. Salvation is free, but oh, the price Jesus paid so I could be redeemed. Thank You. Thank You. Thank You.

O Lord, how great are thy works!
—Psalm 92:5a

FEBRUARY 8

I love watching clouds, observing sunrises, and chasing sunsets. And I'm not quiet about it, either! One morning on the way to school, my then-8 year old grandson exclaimed, "Gramma, look at the sky!" Sunbeams had burst from clouds like a series of spotlights. It really was spectacular, and I said so. He said, "Yeah, and I never noticed stuff like that before I met you." I laughed because, let's face it, that was a cute comment, but deep down I rejoiced. He is noticing God's creation. He is recognizing the beauty around Him.

I think when we notice and exclaim over the touches of wonder God places in our pathway every day, we please Him. His work is awe-inspiring! Let Him know you appreciate it.

---

*Heavenly Father, You created this world and everything on it.
You could have made it meet our physical needs for survival
and left it at that, but You incorporated beauty to entrance us.
Thank You for doing more than enough.
May I never look past the glory of Your creation.*

> *For thou, O God, hast proved us:*
> *thou hast tried us, as silver is tried.*
> —Psalm 66:10

FEBRUARY 9

I read somewhere that to purify silver it must experience extremely high temperatures for a long period of time. A silversmith was asked how he knew when the silver had been purified, and he replied, "When I can see my reflection in it."

This is such a powerful metaphor of God's refining process in our lives. We will encounter "fires" in life, but if we allow those experiences to deepen our trust in Him and use it as an opportunity to show others where we find our strength, then we reflect Him. Remembering the silversmith's comment helps change my attitude about difficult times. Shine, Christian, shine!

Heavenly Father, although the fires are painful,
thank You for their refining purpose.
May every trial and every heartache hold a heavenly purpose
of drawing me closer to You and better reflecting You
to a world who needs Your truth.

> *But verily God hath heard me; he hath attended to the voice of my prayer.*
> —Psalm 66:19

FEBRUARY 10

When my girls were babies, I learned the meaning of their different cries. I could differentiate between a hungry cry, an "I'm wet" cry, a cry of pain, and a cry of boredom. I'm just a human mom, so how much more must God—who is perfect in every way—recognize the sounds of our prayers? He knows exactly what we're feeling, exactly what we need, and as a loving Father He listens and responds to our prayers in the way that's best for us. He's listening—share your heart with Him.

*Heavenly Father, thank You for never turning a deaf ear to my cries.
Thank You for answering in Your perfect time
and in a way that's best for me.
Thank You for being such a good, good Father.*

But now ye also put off all these; anger, wrath, malice, blasphemy, filthy communication out of your mouth. Lie not one to another, seeing that ye have put off the old man with his deeds; And have put on the new man, which is renewed in knowledge after the image of him that created him:
—Colossians 3:8-10

FEBRUARY 11

Out with the old, in with the new...that's what happens when we accept Jesus. The Holy Spirit indwells us. All the ugly sin nature—anger, slander, foul language, untruthfulness—has no place in us anymore. Instead, we become renewed according to the image of our Creator. How does this happen? By increasing our knowledge. How do we increase our knowledge? By studying His Word and seeking His wisdom.

If there's some ugly ol' sin nature still hanging around, talk to Him and ask for His help to eradicate it. He never says no to our honest petitions to grow more like Him.

*Heavenly Father, thank You for saving me.
Please work in me to rid me of any attitudes or habits
that harm me or damage my testimony.
Dear Father, make me new so I might be like You.*

> *And whatsoever ye do in word or deed,*
> *do all in the name of the Lord Jesus,*
> *giving thanks to God and the Father by him.*
> —Colossians 3:17

FEBRUARY 12

I'm sure this is a familiar verse to all of you. "Whatever you do..." Big things, little things, simple things, complicated things—whatever it is you set your hand to, be grateful for the opportunity and do it to serve Him. Little is much when God is in it. We never know what kind of impact we can leave when we turn our hearts to doing His will.

Heavenly Father, as I go about my daily duties,
help me to quell a complaining spirit
and instead see my tasks as an offering to You.

But as many as received him, to them gave he power to become the sons of God, even to them that believe on his name:
—John 1:12

FEBRUARY 13

What a joy and privilege to call God our Father! Not everyone has an earthly father—sometimes fathers die; sometimes they walk away; sometimes they refuse any part of responsibility toward their children. But we can all have a heavenly Father who will never leave us, never abandon us, always give us everything we need. Of all my "titles," child of the King is my favorite!

Heavenly Father, You are the Father to the fatherless.
You love unconditionally and You promise
to never leave us nor forsake us.
Thank You for the opportunity to become Your children—
heirs with Jesus, secure forevermore.

> *Now when they saw the boldness of Peter and John, and perceived that they were unlearned and ignorant men, they marveled; and they took knowledge of them, that they had been with Jesus.*
> —Acts 4:13

FEBRUARY 14

The religious leaders saw something different in Peter and John, and they realized that the difference came because these men had been with Jesus. When we have been with Jesus, it shows. We treat people with greater compassion. We exhibit honesty and morality. We choose patience instead of anger, forgiveness instead of revenge. We reflect *Him*. And what a difference we make when we let it be seen that we have been with Jesus.

Heavenly Father, in this world with its negative examples and pitfalls, hold me close and keep me from straying. How I want to show the world the difference You make in a person's life.

> ...all men glorified God for that which was done. For the man was above forty years old, on whom this miracle of healing was shewed.
> —Acts 21b-22

FEBRUARY 15

Has anyone ever tried to refute your faith? If it hasn't happened yet, it will. Rather than arguing, there's a simple response that no one can deny: your own testimony. The Sanhedrin couldn't deny that a man who'd been crippled since birth was now standing and walking.

You know what brokenness God has healed in your life. You know the times He's provided for you. You know the comfort or peace or wisdom He's given. Your testimony is *your testimony*, and it points to the presence and care of a loving Father-God. So when questioned, proclaim it! No one can deny the truth of your changed life.

Heavenly Father, thank You for being the Healer and Restorer.
You are my Strength and my Confidence.
I know I am nothing without You.
Thank You for opportunities to proclaim You.
May I do so boldly and joyfully.

> *And now, Lord, behold their threatenings: and grant unto thy servants, that with all boldness they may speak thy word*
> —Acts 4:29

FEBRUARY 16

It's flat out not easy to be a Christian. People will reject you, hurl accusations at you, or ridicule you. But that doesn't mean we should hush or change our behavior to match the world. Especially in this time when our religious freedoms are being trampled by those who are offended by anything that speaks of Jesus, we need to be bold and stand for what is right. Elsewhere in Acts 4, Peter tells the religious leaders, "Judge for yourself whether it is right in God's sight to obey you rather than God." Follow your heart (your moral compass) and your conscience (the Holy Spirit), dear Christian, when facing conflict. God will embolden you to speak truth, and He will bless you for honoring Him.

Heavenly Father, You do so much for me.
Give me the courage and the true yet loving words to speak
in defense of You when the need arises.

That if thou shalt confess with thy mouth the Lord Jesus, and shalt believe in thine heart that God hath raised him from the dead, thou shalt be saved.
—Romans 10:9

FEBRUARY 17

Becoming a Christian is very simple: Believe on the Lord and you will be saved. But then we need to go to a deeper level. There are a lot of people who will say, "I believe there's a God," or "I believe Jesus was born," but their declarations are "lip service." There's no heart involvement. If you believe in your heart that Jesus came to this earth to die *for you*, then your life will reflect your gratitude. A good self-examination: If you were arrested for being a Christian, would there be enough evidence to convict you? Jesus on the inside will show on the outside.

Heavenly Father, in this lost and full-of-darkness world, let Your light shine through me.

> *Thou calledst in trouble,*
> *and I delivered thee;*
> *I answered thee*
> *in the secret place of thunder:*
> —Psalm 81:7

FEBRUARY 18

I don't know the title or singer of the song, but every now and then as I listen to Christian radio, I hear this snippet of lyric: "I find you in the hurricane." And I always smile. When I look back at my life, the times when I most felt the Father's presence was in the middle of the darkest storms. Maybe it's my fault. When things are going well, I don't seek Him the way I should. But when things are tough? That's when I cry out for Him. And y'know what? He always answers. Even as the thunder roars and winds howl and waves pummel my little boat, He's there. I don't have to face the storm alone.

Heavenly Father, thank You for never leaving me to face a storm alone. You don't always calm the storm, but You always calm Your child.

That in every thing ye are enriched by him, in all utterance, and in all knowledge;
—1 Corinthians 1:5

FEBRUARY 19

A lot of people struggle with insecurity. They view themselves as inept or unworthy. Consequently they don't believe they can accomplish anything of value. That mindset is so wrong! Christians are endowed with the strength they need to live triumphantly for Christ and be a witness to His reality. Do not ever believe the devil's whisper that you are incapable of accomplishing good. God's word clearly says otherwise.

---

*Heavenly Father, thank You for seeing my value—
equal to the life of Your Son.
Please silence the negative voice that tells me I'm unworthy
and let me hear Your voice of truth.*

> Help me, O Lord my God:
> O save me according to thy mercy:
> That they may know that this is thy
> hand; that thou, LORD, hast done it.
> —Psalm 100:26-27

FEBRUARY 20

Some of my fondest memories are of taking walks with my oldest daughter when she was a toddler. A walk around the block could take an hour because she examined everything. Her intense scrutiny caused me to truly look, too, and I marveled at the intricacy of our world. Who but God could create something as delicate as the veins in a leaf or the tiny clustered petals of a dandelion bloom?

Years ago a friend's grandbaby, who'd been diagnosed with a syndrome that causes the intestines to form outside the body, was born perfectly healthy. The doctor who delivered her said, "This never happens." Nature couldn't reconstruct that baby girl's body, but God could. There was no doubt in anyone's mind that God had worked a miracle. I love it when things happen that cannot be explained any other way than "thou, LORD, hast done it."

*Heavenly Father, thank You for miracles
that prove Your presence.
May I never doubt Your ability to heal and save.*

*Bring my soul out of prison,
that I may praise thy name...*
—Psalm 147:7a

FEBRUARY 21

Have you ever felt trapped in a prison of circumstance? Life in this fallen world sometimes places us in uncomfortable or hurtful settings. There is one way to release our soul from the dark, lonely cell: praise. When we praise His name, we invite His presence to encompass us. When He encompasses us, peace that defies understanding descends. We are released from despair to a place of "it is well with my soul." Sometimes there isn't much we can do about where life takes us, but there is always something we can do about how we handle it. Will you pout...or praise?

---

*Heavenly Father, develop in me the ability to praise You
for who You are even when circumstances are troubling.
You, my Lord, are my Strength and my Song.*

God is faithful, by whom ye were called unto the fellowship of his Son Jesus Christ our Lord.
—1 Corinthians 1:9

FEBRUARY 22

In my years of life, there have been many, many times when people have disappointed me, crushed me, abandoned me. But God has not. He is always faithful. Even when I don't understand why hardships come or why my prayers are answered with a no instead of the exultant yes for which I long, I still know...He is faithful. The longer I walk with Him, the more I see His faithfulness.

Rest assured, Christian sister or brother, He will always be there to love you, guide you, encourage you, strengthen you. You are never alone.

Heavenly Father, thank You for Your promise to be with me. Help me lean on You when times are hard and let me grow in grace through every trial.

We are troubled on every side, yet not distressed; we are perplexed, but not in despair; Persecuted, but not forsaken; cast down, but not destroyed;
—2 Corinthians 4:8-9

FEBRUARY 23

Life can be tough. Challenges attack. Sorrows descend. But when we remember that we have hope, life's difficulties become secondary to the victory that is already ours.

My youngest daughter suffered brain damage from oxygen deprivation at birth. She went through extensive therapy, and I battled through anger, fear, and sorrow. I was definitely cast down, but thanks to having learned through previous life events to lean on God's strength, I was not destroyed.

His strength sustains us in the most difficult trials. No matter how dim it seems on earth, we know that Jesus has overcome the world.

---

*Heavenly Father, You are not a wasteful God.
Everything in my life can benefit me spiritually
and give me an opportunity to shine Your grace.
So thank You for making beauty from ashes.*

For which cause we faint not; but though our outward man perish, yet the inward man is renewed day by day. For our light affliction, which is but for a moment, worketh for us a far more exceeding and eternal weight of glory; While we look not at the things which are seen, but at the things which are not seen: for the things which are seen are temporal; but the things which are not seen are eternal.
—2 Corinthians 4:16-18

FEBRUARY 24

Can you say "I have no trials or hardships in my life right now"? If so, enjoy it. It likely won't last. I don't say that to defeat you, but just to remind you that this world brings trouble. It is fallen, and people are still trapped in sin. But the difficulties we are facing today, no matter how dark or heartbreaking, cannot compare to what awaits us in Heaven. So don't give up! Use hardships as an opportunity to deepen your dependence on Christ. Let trials serve as a means of showing others how Jesus strengthens us. Don't focus on the seen: the present challenge, but on the unseen: the place God has prepared for us. These troubles are temporary. Our joy will be eternal.

---

*Heavenly Father, thank You
for holding the victory over sin and death.
Remind me in times of doubt that this life is temporal;
eternity is forever, and I will spend it with You.*

> *He trusted in the LORD God of Israel; so that after him was none like him among all the kings of Judah, nor any that were before him.*
> —2 Kings 18:5

FEBRUARY 25

Am I the only weird person who sits at funerals and wonders how her own will turn out? Or, more accurately, what kind of "turn out" I'll have? Will they say good things about me when I'm gone? Those thoughts lead me to pondering if I'm wasting the limited hours I have on this earth. I love what is said here about Hezekiah— He trusted the LORD God; he was unlike any king that preceded or followed him. Apparently Hezekiah left his positive mark on the world. As Christians, our foremost goal should be to leave a mark that leads others to eternity. This starts with unwavering faith in God. Deep faith affects our behavior, actions, and attitude.

Heavenly Father, let me trust You more and more.

Commit thy way unto the Lord; trust also in him; and he shall bring it to pass. And he shall bring forth thy righteousness as the light, and thy judgment as the noonday.
—Psalm 37:5-6

FEBRUARY 26

Faith starts with a simple declaration: I will follow You. When we commit our way to Him, when we trust His guidance, He can work in us and through us. He can mold us to more greatly reflect Him. This world is shrouded in the darkness of sin, but we can be a beacon of light that points to Him.

---

*Heavenly Father, lead me and guide me;
let me closely follow You.*

Trust in him at all times; ye people, pour out your heart before him: God is a refuge for us.
—Psalm 62:8

FEBRUARY 27

I read about a wire-walker who wowed crowds by successfully walking back and forth across Niagara Falls. On his return, he grabbed a wheelbarrow and asked the audience if they believed he could push the wheelbarrow across the wire. They all roared their assurances. Then he said, "Who would like to ride in the wheelbarrow?" And no one stepped forward.

Trust is faith in action. If we really believe God is our refuge, then we will give Him our deepest hurts and concerns. We will trustingly climb "into the wheelbarrow" and rest in His arms.

---

*Lord, let me hold nothing back from You
but give You every part of me for Your service and glory.*

> *Behold, God is my salvation; I will trust, and not be afraid: for the LORD JEHOVAH is my strength and my song; he also is become my salvation.*
> —Isaiah 12:2

FEBRUARY 28

I have a timid kitty named Clyde. He is afraid of everything: strangers, loud noises, a shoe left in the middle of the floor that wasn't there an hour ago… I've tried so hard to be gentle with him, to assure him he's safe here in our house, but he remains skittish and on alert. My heart aches when I watch him; I wish so much he could relax and feel at ease.

I wonder if this is how God feels when we live our lives in fear and uncertainty, constantly watching for the next "attack" rather than trusting Him to take care of us? We can say "I have faith in God," but unless we put that faith into action—unless we exhibit trust—then they're only words.

Heavenly Father, take my fears and help me rest in Your strength. Let my heartfelt song always be "great is Thy faithfulness."

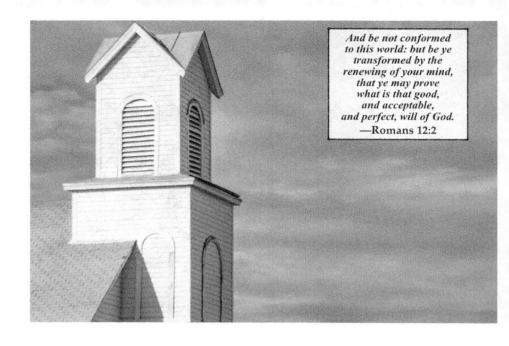

And be not conformed to this world: but be ye transformed by the renewing of your mind, that ye may prove what is that good, and acceptable, and perfect, will of God.
—Romans 12:2

FEBRUARY 29

I'm always captured by the reflection of the sky on water. It makes the entire world appear the same glorious shade that graces the sky. But Christians need to be careful about picking up the "colors" of the world. It can be so easy to adopt the attitudes, habits, and mindset of "the majority." Before we accept an idea as right, we need to weigh it against God's Word. His precepts are our measuring stick, not the popular practices, not the noisy protesters, not even the laws passed by our state and federal leaders. Christians are to seek God's wisdom. We do this by studying the Bible, by seeking Him in prayer, by striving to follow Him. Don't be deceived by the world's shouts; obey God's whisper.

*Heavenly Father, the world shouts its desires,
and it's easy to lose Your voice in the chaos.
Tune my heart to hear Your truth,
and let my life glorify You in the choices I make.*

> *Let love be without dissimulation.*
> *Abhor that which is evil;*
> *cleave to that which is good.*
> —Romans 12:9

MARCH 1

A lot of people have a hard time separating sinners from the sin. Instead of attacking the problem, they attack the person. This is opposite of what God instructs us to do. We are to sincerely love others the way Christ loved us. Christ didn't wait for people to become perfect and then love them; He loved them where they were—dirty and lost and shameful. But He loved them too much to leave them in that state.

When we cling to what is good (God), we are given the ability to love bigger and better. When we love sinners, they are drawn to us and to our Savior. Sin is ugly and separates people from God, so it's to be hated. But Christ loved so much, He died for sinners. We are called to follow His example.

Heavenly Father, thank You for loving me—
even the unlovable parts of me.
Please give me Your eyes of grace to look past the sin
to the sinner and love with Your love
so the lost might be drawn into
a life-changing relationship with You.

*Rejoicing in hope;
patient in tribulation;
continuing instant in prayer;*
—Romans 12:12

MARCH 2

Do you know someone who just seems to "shine" Jesus? Chances are this person is one who has found the ability to hold joyfully to hope, to wait patiently for God's answer in times of hardship, and to whom prayer is an natural as breathing. Do you ever think, "I wish I could be more like (fill-in-the-name)"? There's no secret formula involved. We can all possess these attributes. It comes through faith. It comes through spending more time with God. It comes through clinging even more firmly to the One who loves us. The closer we are to Him, the more we reflect Him. So hold tight, dear Christian, and allow Him to flood you with His grace, peace, strength, and purpose.

*Heavenly Father, thank You for Your hope, which is always mine.
May I prayerfully trust You to bring about Your perfect will
in every situation in my life.*

> *Be not overcome of evil,*
> *but overcome evil with good.*
> —Romans 12:21

MARCH 3

I once heard someone teasingly twist the Golden Rule in this way: "Do unto others before they do unto you." It made me giggle, but maybe it isn't such a laughing matter. There are too many who live by that kind of guide rule. Some do it as a means of protecting themselves; others find pleasure in causing another person pain. But as Christians we are advised to resist giving in to evil ways.

When someone else is evil, rather than repaying them in like manner, we need to show them kindness. My mom used to tell me, "If someone acts ugly it's because they feel ugly inside. Instead of getting mad at them, pity them. And pray for them." She gave good advice. They will know we are Christians by our love.

Heavenly Father, in moments when temptation grips me
to lash out in retaliation, please guard my tongue and my attitude.
Build in me the ability to exhibit Your compassion and mercy.

*Teach me thy way, O Lord;
I will walk in thy truth:
unite my heart to fear thy name.*
—Psalm 86:11

MARCH 4

It has been said there are no atheists in foxholes. When in tremendous need, when greatly fear-filled, suddenly we want to believe there is Someone bigger and stronger and wiser who can help us face the trial. Perhaps, then, this is why troubles come our way. To let us learn to seek His counsel and build our faith in His presence. Teach me Your way...that's a good prayer for all of us.

---

*Heavenly Father, thank You for the lessons of life
that teach me to lean into You and grow in faith.
Grow in me a habit of looking to You
in times of trial and heartache.*

And in very deed for this cause have I raised thee up, for to shew in thee my power; and that my name may be declared throughout all the earth.
—Exodus 9:16

MARCH 5

Several years ago, a dear saint named Diann Hunt graduated to Glory after a courageous fight with cancer. I hate cancer, and I hated that this woman—this lovely, vivacious, oh-so-loved woman—contracted the disease. But I can honestly say Diann taught me a great deal about leaning on the Lord's strength, about maintaining a positive outlook in the hardest time, about refusing to let go of hope. God prepared her for that battle, and she prepared herself by walking faithfully at His side from the time she was a small child. In her witness, I saw evidence of His power in human flesh, and He was glorified through her life.

We all have a purpose, and showing Him to others is our greatest purpose. Stand strong, dear Christian. This world needs to see the Father glorified.

Heavenly Father, thank You for growing me strong
and secure in Your love.
Let my life bear testimony to Your presence
and be a witness to Your strength in times of heartache.

> But let patience have her perfect work, that ye may be perfect and entire, wanting nothing.
> —James 1:4

MARCH 6

The Hubs joined the military one year into our marriage. Boot camp nearly did him in. Midway through he wanted to come home, but he stuck it out and later he said he was glad he stayed. The sometimes over-zealous discipline of boot camp prepared him for his military career. Likewise, God's discipline prepares us for this journey called life. We have to stay on faith's pathway; we have to hold tight to His hand. Our perseverance builds maturity and leads us to the place of peace regardless of circumstances. Trials aren't fun, but they serve a wonderful purpose—building our strength for the good of the Kingdom.

Heavenly Father, thank You for Your loving discipline that leads me to Godly character.
May I always look to You as my Guide and Advisor.

But as for me, my prayer is unto thee, O Lord, in an acceptable time: O God, in the multitude of thy mercy hear me, in the truth of thy salvation.
—Psalm 69:13

MARCH 7

Have you ever prayed and prayed and prayed for someone's affliction to be lifted, yet the person continued to suffer? It's hard, isn't it? But consider this: The moon has no light of its own; it can only reflect the sun. The darker the night, the brighter the moon looks. And it occurs to me...the darker the situation, the greater the opportunity to shine Jesus to those around us, to beam faith and trust and hope. So maybe, just maybe, when God doesn't answer our prayers to lift that affliction the way *we* want it lifted, He has a greater purpose. And faith is trusting Him to answer in His time in the way that is best for the person we love, for us, and for all who might be watching for a glimpse of the Savior.

---

*Heavenly Father, thank You for never leaving me
to face trials alone and for giving me the strength to endure.
Help me reflect Your Son in the way I handle life's challenges.*

*I will praise thy name,
O Lord;
for it is good.*
—Psalm 54:6b

MARCH 8

I am a gasper. When I see something spectacular, like a shimmering rainbow, I gasp. It drives my husband crazy—he says, "You scare me when you do that!" But I can't help it. All this happiness wells inside of me and spills out in a delight-filled gasp.

Rainbows speak to me. I see them as God's promises painted across the sky in bright bands of color. Each color holds special meaning, too—purple for royalty, red for Christ's redeeming blood, green for new life, yellow for the Son... So when I see a rainbow, first I gasp, then I praise.

---

*Heavenly Father, thank You for Your promises—
to give me grace, to give me strength, to never leave me.
You keep Your promises from everlasting to everlasting.
You are my stability in an unstable world.
I praise You for who You are!*

> *Give me understanding, and I shall keep thy law; yea, I shall observe it with my whole heart.*
> —Psalm 119:34

MARCH 9

Sometimes I wish God would paint a billboard across the sky so I would know, without a doubt, exactly what I'm meant to do. But y'know, what we do have at our disposal is His Word. And He promises that he who asks for wisdom receives it. I guess instead of wishing for billboards I should stick my nose in the Bible, where it says I will find Him if I seek Him with all my heart. Answers await!

---

*Heavenly Father, thank You for Your Word,
where wisdom and encouragement and guidance
is always available to me.
May I apply it for my good and Your glory.*

Yea, though I walk through the valley of the shadow of death, I will fear no evil: for thou art with me; thy rod and thy staff they comfort me.
—Psalm 23:4

MARCH 10

I do *not* like spiders. They scare me. Badly. If we took a "what scares you?" poll, everyone would be able to list at least one thing they find frightening. Sometimes fear is a good thing—it keeps us from being unduly reckless or from entering a situation which common sense dictates as threatening. But other times fear keeps us from living life fully.

Whatever our fears, God offers comfort. He gives us strength to move forward when our trembling limbs resist progress. He doesn't want us caught up in a net of fear. In our darkest, most difficult times, all we have to do is call His name…and we are not alone.

Heavenly Father, thank You for Your presence at all times in life. Help me choose faith over fear.

> *It is better to trust in the LORD than to put confidence in man.*
> —Psalm 118:8

MARCH 11

Sometimes, because we're trapped in human skin and our humanity gets in the way, Christians don't act very Christ-like. Unfortunately, those who aren't believers then look at the unChrist-like behavior as "proof" that God doesn't really exist or make a difference in a person's life.

I could refute that, but I think there's better advice: Don't look at people. Look at God. Look at Jesus. Allow the Holy Spirit to impact your life. Humans will disappoint you every time. God's righteousness won't allow Him to do anything less than what is good. Jesus, though tempted, emerged triumphant. The Holy Spirit won't lead you astray. So use the Father, Son, and Spirit as your examples to follow, and your feet will be secure.

Heavenly Father, thank You for Your goodness, for Jesus's faithfulness, and the Spirit's guidance. May I strive to emulate You in how I live my life.

Not forsaking the assembling of ourselves together, as the manner of some is; but exhorting one another: and so much the more, as ye see the day approaching.
—Hebrews 10:25

MARCH 12

When I look at majestic mountains, thick forests of trees, or a carpet of delicate flowers, I see the Maker. I'm sure you do, too. The wonder and awe of creation fills me, and I can't help but turn my focus heavenward and praise God for His amazing creation. But does that moment of admiration and praise replace worshiping with fellow believers? No. God knows we need the support and encouragement and even the accountability of a body of believers to help us stay true to our faith.

Yes, you can worship alone on a mountaintop, but remember to meet with and encourage your fellow believers, too. We need each other as evil runs rampant and the day of Christ's return approaches.

Heavenly Father, thank You for the Body of Christ and the role it plays in my personal growth and edification. May I be an encouraging member of Your church.

As for God, his way is perfect: the word of the Lord is tried: he is a buckler to all those that trust in him.
—Psalm 18:30

MARCH 13

God is our buckler—our Defender. In ancient days, a buckler was a shield that covered the entire body. Rocks and arrows glanced off of it so the wearer was protected.

When we put our full trust in Him, we are secure from Satan's darts. We know we can trust Him because His word is proven and true. His ways are perfect because He is all-knowing and wise. Of all the "security systems" available in the world, God is our greatest source of security. We have access to a greater power source than anything this world can offer—we have God the Father.

---

*Heavenly Father, thank You for being my buckler,
my shield and defender.
Let me confidently follow You.*

Thou wilt keep him in perfect peace, whose mind is stayed on thee: because he trusteth in thee.
—Isaiah 26:3

MARCH 14

This is one of my go-to verses when the weight of the world and its heartbreaking inhumanities try to drag me under. When we truly trust God's love, compassion, and provision, we find a place of peace. Circumstances can't destroy us because we know He already holds the victory over today's challenges. When worry nibbles and fear descends, turn your eyes on Him. He who trusts...rests peacefully.

Heavenly Father, thank You for being trustworthy.
Thank You for the gift of peace.
May I love and serve You with my heart, soul, and mind.

A word fitly spoken is like apples of gold in pictures of silver.
—Proverbs 25:11

MARCH 15

When I took classes to become an elementary teacher, a professor gave us a sage piece of advice: Be careful what you say to children; it takes twelve positive comments to overcome one negative one.

I'm sure we've all found this to be true. One unkind word can shatter us. Perhaps that's why God advised His children in the book of James and other places in the Bible to exercise caution before speaking. Today, this extends to the Internet, which makes it far too easy to share something that could cause pain to someone else. Wise words, edifying words, words of truth and kindness—these are the words God calls us to speak.

*Heavenly Father, guard my tongue
and let me speak words of truth, of life,
of encouragement, of edification.
Father, let my words point others to You.*

He is thy praise, and he is thy God, that hath done for thee these great and terrible things, which thine eyes have seen.
—Deuteronomy 10:21

MARCH 16

Life sometimes feels as if we're sailing downhill. The pace, the busyness, and the distractions all keep us from seeing the wonder of God's work in and around us. He is always at work in nature, in relationships, in individual hearts and minds. Pause for a moment and reflect on God's work in you—comforting you, strengthening you, answering your prayers, meeting your needs. Praise Him for the things He has done. A heart of gratitude is something we all should cultivate. He is your God! Praise Him.

---

*Heavenly Father, thank You for all You do for me.
Let me be more aware of Your workings
and more appreciative of Your attention.*

And lest thou lift up thine eyes unto heaven, and when thou seest the sun, and the moon, and the stars, even all the host of heaven, shouldest be driven to worship them, and serve them, which the Lord thy God hath divided unto all nations under the whole heaven.
—Deuteronomy 4:19

MARCH 17

So often I find myself mesmerized by clouds or sunbeams or a rainbow or a towering tree or a delicate flower or a butterfly or... This could go on and on, but I'll stop there.

It would be easy to sing praises for the sky, but I have to be careful that I only sing praises to the Maker of the sky. When I allow the created to overshadow the Creator, I am engaging in idolatry, something that God warns against. There is much beauty in this world and many things that inspire our admiration, but only One is worthy of our awe.

Heavenly Father, thank You for the beauty of creation.
May my heart look beyond the created to You,
the Creator, and revere You above all else.

*Who covereth the heaven with clouds,
who prepareth rain for the earth,
who maketh grass to grow upon the mountains.*
—Psalm 147:8

MARCH 18

The Maker of the universe did something very specific when He was crafting this world—He arranged to meet our needs. He brings rain to nourish the soil. He grows grass and plants to feed the creatures. He provides materials so we can be sheltered. And, best of all, He spreads His love over us, a love that is deeper and wider and more unconditional than words can explain. Whatever we need, in His lovingkindness, He gives it. Isn't He an amazing Father?

---

*Heavenly Father, thank You for Your provision.
I shall not want because I trust in You.*

Praise ye the LORD.
Praise God in his sanctuary:
praise him in the firmament of his power.
—Psalm 150:1

MARCH 19

Have you ever had a grumpy day? I think all of us wake up on the "wrong side" of the bed now and then. Makes for a miserable day…for us and for those we encounter (*grin*).

There's an antidote to the grumpies: praise. When we are honest with ourselves, there's always something for which to be grateful. Can circumstances steal your soul from Him? Can circumstances change who He is to you? Absolutely not. When I balance today's troubles against the promise of eternity, suddenly a praise song builds in my heart.

Hallelujah! Praise Him! It'll change your entire outlook.

Heavenly Father, thank You for loving me even on my grumpy days.
Grow in me a heart of praise that sees Your good
regardless of circumstances.
May I ever praise Your holy, worthy Name.

...can any understand the spreadings of the clouds, or the noise of his tabernacle?
—Job 36:29

MARCH 20

One of my go-to reminders when times are tough is that eternity is waiting for those who call God "Father." In the meantime, because we are stuck down here in a sinful world, it's hard not to question why things are happening the way they are...especially when "things" have a negative trickle-over on you. But here's the thing—God works in ways that we cannot see. I don't know how He crafted those clouds from mists of evaporation. I don't understand how a flash of lightning can result in a rolling rumble of thunder. And I don't have to understand to appreciate that my Father is with me, to accept that He knows best, and to trust Him with my worries and cares and heartaches. The God who created this vast universe can certainly take care of me...and you.

---

*Heavenly Father, You crafted this world
and everything in it, including me.
Thank You for always having my best interest at heart.
Let me trust You even when I don't understand.*

*I am the true vine,
and my Father is the
husbandman.
Every branch in me
that beareth not fruit
he taketh away:
and every branch
that beareth fruit,
he purgeth it, that it may
bring forth more fruit.
Now ye are clean
through the word
which I have spoken unto you.
Abide in me, and I in you.
As the branch cannot bear fruit
of itself, except it abide
in the vine;
no more can ye,
except ye abide in me.*
—John 15:1-4

MARCH 21

I love reading Jesus's words to His disciples. Those words are for us, too! I also love how often He used metaphorical language, turning His teaching into a story-like quality. These verses about the vine and branches are a prime example of that. A good vineyard owner knows the plant must be pruned in order for it to bear greater fruit. Our Father-God knows He needs to prune those things from our lives that would harm us spiritually. Have you ever faced the "pruning" process? It can be painful, but the end result is always worth it. When we stay in tune with Jesus and His teachings, we're less likely to need "trimming," and the fruit we bear will bring glory to Him. Doesn't get much better than that.

---

*Heavenly Father, thank You for Your pruning
that results in my bearing greater fruit.
May I grow ever deeper in faith and trust
and bring glory to You, my Lord and Maker.*

...he giveth to all life, and breath, and all things;
—Acts 17:25b

MARCH 22

The "all things" of this verse used to trouble me. Did God give me heartaches and difficulties? Some may disagree with me, and that's okay, but I've come to the conclusion that as long as I'm living in a fallen world, I'm going to encounter pain. God allows that pain as a teaching tool.

When I'm weak, He's strong; when I'm distressed, He comforts me. Every challenge gives me an opportunity to show how leaning on Him is better than depending on myself.

He gives us so much: life, breath, and Himself to guide us through the pathways of life.

---

*Heavenly Father, thank You for always bearing me up.
Let me see hardship not as a pitfall
but as an opportunity to grow in grace and trust.*

> *Blessed are they that keep his testimonies, and that seek him with the whole heart.*
> *They also do no iniquity: they walk in his ways.*
> —Psalm 119:2-3

MARCH 23

Have you ever noticed that those who seem to have the "most"—i.e., wealth, power, fame—can also seem to be least happy? If these people had joy in the center of their souls, they wouldn't use drugs or alcohol or take their own lives. The key to joy is found within these verses.

Those who know God and strive to live as He directed have a deep down satisfaction the world and its pleasures cannot give. When we walk without sin, we walk free of regret and the painful consequences of poor choices. A sad-faced Christian is a poor billboard. If you've lost your joy, perhaps you've gotten caught up in the world or entangled yourself in legalistic practices that only mimic true love for God. There's a simple antidote: Look for Him with all your heart. Those who seek Him will find Him, and He will restore you.

Heavenly Father, thank You for being the giver of joy.
May I constantly seek You first,
and may my life be a testimony of holiness.

I will meditate in thy precepts, and have respect unto thy ways.
—Psalm 119:15

MARCH 24

When God put man on the earth, He gave us two basic laws by which to live: first, love the Lord your God with all your heart; and second, love your neighbor as yourself. Such elementary precepts, simple enough for a child to comprehend. Yet we ignore them, choosing to think of ourselves and therefore showing disrespect for others. So many heartaches could be avoided if people used God's law as their "rules to live by."

Christian, let us make a concerted effort to follow God's laws and be a beacon of His love. Love changes people from the inside out.

Heavenly Father, thank You for wanting the best for mankind. Let me follow Your guidelines in loving You most, because then loving others will be a natural outgrowth of You flowing through me.

My soul melteth for heaviness: strengthen thou me according unto thy word.
—Psalm 119:28

MARCH 25

Man's inhumanity toward man has always been a source of heartache and confusion, and my soul aches for lives affected by violence and hatred. But I've also found a source of comfort: God's Word. God is still my Father. I find peace when I set my mind on Him. No matter what happens here, I have the hope of eternity waiting. Regardless of what conflicts and trials happen around me, Jesus still holds the victory. It might be dark right now, but I know joy comes in the morning.

We find our strength in our faith in Him while we pray for Him to comfort those who are hurting and to change the hearts of those who choose to do harm. We also find comfort in knowing how many of our Christian brothers and sisters are praying, too. The prayers of the righteous avail much! Hold to hope—He's still on His throne.

---

*Heavenly Father, You give strength to the weak
and embolden the powerless.
Strengthen and embolden me to set an example
of Your grace in this hurting, mixed up world.*

For God, who commanded the light to shine out of darkness, hath shined in our hearts, to give the light of the knowledge of the glory of God in the face of Jesus Christ.
—2 Corinthians 4:6

MARCH 26

When you're driving across the Kansas countryside, you might look at what's growing in a field and wonder what kind of crop it is, but when it's a field of sunflowers, you *know*. Their round, yellow, happy faces announce themselves without saying a word.

By the same token, when you look across a room full of people, you should be able to determine who are followers of Christ. You should see Him shining through in their countenance, in the way they speak, in the way they treat others. In these days of turmoil, people desperately need to see Christ reflected. We are His glory—shine, Christian, shine!

---

*Heavenly Father, thank You for Your word,
which gives me knowledge.
Please let Your countenance glow in me
so others might see You in the things I say and do.*

...the trial of your faith, being much more precious than of gold that perisheth, though it be tried with fire, might be found unto praise and honour and glory at the appearing of Jesus Christ:
—1 Peter 1:7

MARCH 27

The Hubs has a workshop, and when he builds chairs or benches, he tests them to make sure they're strong and secure. Testing involves pulling or thumping or otherwise applying discomfort to the item in question. But the testing proves the strength.

It's the same way with faith. Until it's been put to the test, how can we know if we have it? If we've never been tested, how can we share the truth of God's strength in our lives to unbelievers? There is a purpose in trials—they build spiritual muscle. Praise Him through the storm—your faith will shine.

Heavenly Father, thank You for giving me opportunities to strengthen my spiritual muscles. Let me stand firm in times of conflict and be a witness to the power of faith in You.

Whether therefore ye eat, or drink, or whatsoever ye do, do all to the glory of God.
—1 Corinthians 10:31

MARCH 28

Most times we see only the last half of this verse used. It's kind of strange to reflect on the first half. But then again, maybe not. "You are what you eat," nutritionists say. If I choose healthy food and drink rather than junk, if I choose portions that fill me without overfilling me, then I will be taking better care of myself.

God created me. He placed on the earth the kinds of foods that are good for the body. When I choose wisely and take care of my body, I'm showing respect for God's creation. I want to bring glory to my Father. I pray I make choices that are pleasing to Him.

---

*Heavenly Father, thank You for crafting me in my mother's womb.
May I remember I am Your workmanship
and that my body is Your temple.
Let my choices be ones that glorify You.*

All things are lawful for me, but all things are not expedient: all things are lawful for me, but all things edify not.
—1 Corinthians 10:23

MARCH 29

Today's words might trample a few toes. It's okay—I'm trampling my own toes! The Ten Commandments outline some very clear off-limits things for God's children, but different people see different accountabilities in the other instructions. We have to rely on the Holy Spirit's guidance and not on the world's standard as our measuring stick.

It should be simple: If what I'm doing is lawful but not edifying either for me or for a weaker brother looking on, then I need to pluck it out of my life. My main responsibility as a Christian is to reflect Christ. If my attitude, behavior, or activity fails in that responsibility, it has no place in my life.

Heavenly Father, thank You for the indwelling of the Spirit,
who advises and guides me.
May I heed His voice and make wise decisions
so I never hinder the growth of another brother or sister in Christ.

Wherefore, my dearly beloved, flee from idolatry.
—I Corinthians 10:14

MARCH 30

Chances are none of us have little brass or gold idols to which we bow down and worship, but there are other means of "idolatry" in our lives. Anything that comes before God or interferes with our relationship with Him can be considered an idol. It's a good idea for the Christian to take stock now and then and see if activities or the pursuit of belongings is becoming so important we neglect our time with our Father. If so, flee! He is our greatest satisfaction, so keep Him "front and center."

---

*Heavenly Father, You bless me beyond my deserving.
If anything stands in importance over You,
open my eyes and heart to the change I need to make
so You are the only God in my life.*

There hath no temptation taken you but such as is common to man: but God is faithful, who will not suffer you to be tempted above that ye are able; but will with the temptation also make a way to escape, that ye may be able to bear it.
—1 Corinthians 10:13

MARCH 31

Do any of you remember Flip Wilson? He's a comedian who used to bemoan, "The devil made me do it." Actually, the devil can tempt us, but he can't *make* us do anything; it's our own choice to wallow in sin. God always provides an escape, and it's our responsibility to take it. When we do escape, we can save ourselves from the regret and unpleasant consequences of poor choices. Everyone faces temptation; lean on Him and emerge triumphant.

Heavenly Father, thank You for providing an escape when temptation seizes me. Please empower me to deny temptation and follow Your pathway, where I will find joy and peace.

...he leadeth me in the paths of righteousness for his name's sake.
—Psalm 23:3b

APRIL 1

I have two choices: do my own thing or follow Him. When I'm willing to follow in submission to His will rather than my own, He is faithful to guide me on a path that leads to my joy and peace. When I live a holy life, doing what's right, then I bring glory to my Father. There is no greater joy than walking in His righteousness.

*Heavenly Father, thank You for the path You plan for me,
meant to bring me good and not evil.
May I choose Your will above my own
and be worthy of the title Child of God.*

For therein is the righteousness of God revealed from faith to faith: as it is written, The just shall live by faith.
—Romans 1:17

APRIL 2

If you've accepted Jesus as your Savior, and if you call God Father, then your life should reflect that belief. When we believe, then fear or doubt or worry shouldn't consume us. Instead, faith should be our battle cry. "A man right with God lives by faith." We might not be able to understand, but faith lets us trust even when we cannot see.

---

*Heavenly Father, forgive me when worry takes control.
Help me to cling to You and trust in You
as unconditionally as You love me.*

Before the mountains were brought forth, or ever thou hadst formed the earth and the world, even from everlasting to everlasting, thou art God.
—Psalm 90:2

APRIL 3

God was, God is, God will forever be. Paul wrote to the Corinthians, "For our momentary light affliction is producing for us an absolutely incomparable eternal weight of glory. So we do not focus on what is seen, but on what is unseen. For what is seen is temporary, but what is unseen is eternal." Whatever pain or trial you're suffering today will not last. Everything of this earth comes to an end. But your relationship with God is eternal. Hold tight to Him! He isn't going anywhere.

Heavenly Father, thank You for opening a way for me to know You intimately. Guide and direct me on life's pathways and lead me Home where I will abide with You forevermore.

*Unto thee lift I up mine eyes,
O thou that dwellest in the heavens.*
—Psalm 123:1

APRIL 4

When life is overwhelming—and let's face it, sometimes life is just flat-out hard—is the time to *look up*. "Turn your eyes upon Jesus; look full in His wonderful face. And the things of earth will grow strangely dim in the light of His glory and grace." When my mom was hospitalized before her home-going, we sang that hymn over and over together as a reminder that God is on His throne. He already holds the victory. This world and its troubles are temporary. So look up. Remember the Master of the universe has enough strength to carry us when we can't carry on.

---

*Heavenly Father, thank You for carrying me
when I am too weak to stand on my own.
Thank You for readying a place for me in heaven.
Let me remember in times of sorrow that suffering is temporary,
but You are eternal.*

It is good that a man should both hope and quietly wait for the salvation of the LORD.
—Lamentations 3:26

APRIL 5

Are you in a quandary spot? You know, at a crossroads and uncertain how to proceed? Well then, heed this verse. Wait quietly for the Lord to direct you. He wants to be your Savior and Guide. He has a wonderful plan for your life, and He will reveal it in the perfect time. Our hurry-up-and-go world doesn't exhibit patience for waiting, but God doesn't operate on our time. Be still and wait... He will speak.

Heavenly Father, my hope is in You and You alone.
Give me the patience to trust as I wait
for You to reveal Your full will to me.
As I wait, I praise You for the victory that is already mine.

> *Remembering mine affliction*
> *and my misery, the wormwood and the gall.*
> *My soul hath them still in remembrance,*
> *and is humbled in me. This I recall*
> *to my mind, therefore have I hope.*
> *It is of the Lord's mercies*
> *that we are not consumed,*
> *because his compassions fail not.*
> *—Lamentations 3:19-22*

APRIL 6

None of us make it through this life without encountering hardship. Trials are part of our existence here. But if you've walked with the Lord, you can also look back and see how He guided you through those difficult times. Because we know Him, we always have hope. We always have a ready source of comfort and strength. We are never alone because His compassion for us never fails.

Heavenly Father, Your compassion exceeds my ability to comprehend,
yet I trust that it is there even in my darkest moments.
I will not be consumed by the world's trials
because You hold my hand.

...what doth the LORD thy God require of thee, but to fear the LORD thy God, to walk in all his ways, and to love him, and to serve the LORD thy God with all thy heart and with all thy soul,
—Deuteronomy 10:12

APRIL 7

So many people try to win the Lord's favor by dropping money in an offering plate, performing services, following a man-created list of do-this and don't-do-that, or some other means. But God isn't interested in our works; He's interested in our hearts. When we've committed our heart to Him, then seeing Him in awe, obeying Him, loving Him, and serving Him will intrinsically follow. Set aside the works and put your focus on faith. Relationship—and God-deigned service—will follow.

Heavenly Father, I commit my heart and my will to You. Guide me in the works that will bring glory to Your name and lead me to a place of fulfillment.

To keep the commandments of the Lord, and his statutes, which I command thee this day for thy good?
—Deuteronomy 10:13

APRIL 8

God's laws weren't established so He could "lord" them over us. He gave us guidelines by which to live because He loves us and He knows what's best for us. Loving parents employ expectations for their children so they grow into responsible adults. How much more does our Father-God desire for us to grow into faith-filled vessels? He wants good for us, not despair. When we follow His laws, we can live without regret and self-recrimination. What could be better?

---

*Heavenly Father, thank You for being the attentive, loving Father who always wants the best for me.
Help me walk in Your ways and Your truth all the days of my life.*

And that ye put on the new man, which after God is created in righteousness and true holiness.
—Ephesians 4:24

APRIL 9

Sometimes people don't understand what it means to be holy. They think it means perfect, or goody-goody, or nose-in-the-air. Actually, holiness means "set apart." As believers, we need to live in a way that points unbelievers toward Jesus. Sometimes that can seem an impossible task because we're stuck down here where sin runs rampant and temptation abounds. But there is a way to be holy–by keeping our eyes not on the world, but on Jesus. He provides the guidance, the strength, and the encouragement to keep us on the pathway of righteousness. Stand firm, dear Christian friend, in holiness! This world needs Jesus.

Heavenly Father, I can't be righteous or holy on my own power. Please indwell me and help me live a life worthy of the call of Christ.

If ye endure chastening, God dealeth with you as with sons; for what son is he whom the father chasteneth not?
—Hebrews 12:7

APRIL 10

The word "discipline" is another word often misinterpreted. Sometimes it becomes synonymous with punishment, but that isn't actually the case. Discipline, grown from the root word disciple, is teaching through consistent example and instruction. A loving parent disciplines his children; God, as a loving parent, also disciplines His children. Most of us can probably recall a difficult situation that resulted in growth or strength or another positive result. Consider those situations God's discipline—God's means of molding us into stronger, more empathetic, more usable vessels.

Heavenly Father, thank You for loving me enough to not leave me where I am but to grow me in faith. Thank You for Your hand of discipline constantly molding and directing me.

> *Follow peace with all men, and holiness, without which no man shall see the Lord:*
> —Hebrews 12:14

APRIL 11

One of the saddest statements I've ever heard is, "Christianity is a farce." It's usually made because someone who claims to be a Christian has done something hurtful or inappropriate, leaving an unpleasant taste on an unbeliever's tongue.

First of all, we should never use people as our role model—only Jesus was/is perfect. But second of all, if we claim Christ as Savior, then we should make our best effort to live in a way that reflects Him.

---

*Heavenly Father, never let me behave in a way
that causes a brother or sister to stumble,
or makes a seeking sinner think You don't matter.*

For the king trusteth in the LORD, and through the mercy of the most High he shall not be moved.
—Psalm 21:7

APRIL 12

Security is one of our most basic needs. Children who have no base of security have difficulty trusting people or forming lasting relationships. Nothing in this world can offer a complete sense of security, but the wise king of the Psalms knew where his security source could be found—through the unfailing love of the Most High. Those who rest in His love and strength will not be shaken.

Heavenly Father, thank You for the security You provide. You promise to never leave me nor forsake me, and I fully trust in You.

For the LORD God is a sun and shield: the LORD will give grace and glory: no good thing will he withhold from them that walk uprightly.
—Psalm 84:11

APRIL 13

When we are a child of God, in His eyes, we are holy. Our sins are gone, so we are blameless before Him. As His children, we have access to His presence, which includes His strength, His peace, and His comfort. And one day we will reside with Him...forever and ever and ever! Such wondrous blessings He bestows on those who call Him Father.

---

*Heavenly Father, thank You for making me flawless before You.
If any sin lingers in my heart, please forgive me
so I can stand blameless before You on this day
and on the day when I reach Your throne.*

...for thou hast created all things, and for thy pleasure they are and were created.
—Revelations 4:11b

APRIL 14

By His will, creation was breathed into existence. You are His creation, too! From the beginning of time, He knew you would one day be born, and He knew the number of your days. His care and concern for you are boundless. Isaiah 62:5 even says that God rejoices over you. Does your heart skip a beat with that glorious realization? You are His creation, and as my mom liked to say, God doesn't make junk.

Heavenly Father, thank You for life and breath and purpose.
Thank You for rejoicing over me.
May my actions, attitudes, and accomplishments
bring You pleasure as I strive to do Your will.

The mighty God, even the LORD, hath spoken, and called the earth from the rising of the sun unto the going down thereof.
—Psalm 50:1

APRIL 15

Think about this: God created the earth from nothing. He hung the sun in the sky and gave it the task of warming and lighting the earth but then slipping away so His people could enjoy a peaceful night of sleep. He knew exactly what would be best for us. The Mighty One, our LORD (Yahweh, the Covenant God), knows everything and can do anything. That's why you know you can trust Him with your life.

Heavenly Father, Your greatness is too much for me to comprehend; Your desire to fellowship with me is beyond understanding. Thank You for making me Yours.

> *For what is our hope, or joy, or crown of rejoicing? Are not even ye in the presence of our Lord Jesus Christ at his coming? For ye are our glory and joy.*
> —1 Thessalonians 2:19-20

APRIL 16

Paul wrote a letter to the believers at Thessalonica and shared his love for them, as well as his pride in the way they lived the faith in Jesus Christ to which he'd introduced them. He proclaimed the believers his "glory and joy."

Have you ever stopped to consider that *you* are Jesus' glory and joy? When we live our faith openly, when we show the world through our lives that Jesus makes a difference, we glorify Him and bring Him great joy. Live your faith! Please your Savior, and impact for eternity those you encounter.

---

*Heavenly Father, thank You for creating me,
for redeeming me, for giving me a purpose to fulfill.
May I be Your glory and joy every day I walk this earth.*

To them who by patient continuance in well doing seek for glory and honour and immortality, eternal life:
—Romans 2:7

APRIL 17

There's a wonderful reward waiting those who claim Jesus as Lord and then live to serve Him. Eternity in heaven. As beautiful as this world is, there is nothing here that can compare with what awaits us. Stand firm and keep the faith, brothers and sisters! It will be worth it all when we see Jesus.

*Heavenly Father, thank You for the promise of heaven
and the joy of eternity in Your presence.
Help me stay firm in my faith and use each day wisely
until that time I release my last breath.*

Give unto the Lord the glory due unto his name; worship the Lord in the beauty of holiness.
—Psalm 29:2

APRIL 18

When I was a little girl, I attended church wearing my best dress, with my hair curled and shoes shined. When I entered the sanctuary I knew I was entering God's house, and I behaved respectfully.

Lots of things have changed over the years. Dresses are hard to find, and sometimes I even wear flip-flops (embellished ones!), but there are some things that should never change...such as our humble respect for God. He alone is worthy of praise. When we come into His presence it should be with a hushed expectation that we will experience His splendor. How can I do that if I haven't prepared my heart? Let me never come before Him flippantly. He deserves my best.

---

*Heavenly Father, You are worthy of my praise,
my adoration, my respect, and my awe.
Let me never take You for granted or demean You
with my actions or attitude.*

Be glad in the LORD, and rejoice, ye righteous: and shout for joy, all ye that are upright in heart.
—Psalm 32:11

APRIL 19

We're called to be righteous, but there's no way we can walk morally upright on our own. The world and its temptations constantly pull at our human minds. Good news: we don't have to walk in our own strength. God will give us what we need to emerge triumphant over the world's temptations. Rejoice! Sing His praise! He is there for you this minute, and the next, and the next, and the...

*Heavenly Father, You are ever with me,
and You never leave me struggling against temptation alone!
Thank You for victory over sin.*

That, according as it is written,
He that glorieth, let him glory in the Lord.
—1 Corinthians 1:31

APRIL 20

Humility is recognizing we aren't "all that and a bag of chips." It isn't self-criticism but self-awareness. All of us have certain gifts and talents, and God expects us to use those gifts for His glory rather than our own. After all, He is our Creator. Why should the prairie grasses brag about their bold gold stems or the sky boast about its delicate blue color? The grass and the sky were created by God...so those tall grasses and covering of blue should point to the One who put them in place. Don't put yourself down—you are His creation. Let your life point others to the Creator.

Heavenly Father, may any boasting I do be of You
and the works of Your hand.
May I live in humility before You and men
so that You may be glorified.

For great is the LORD, and greatly to be praised:
—1 Chronicles 16:25a

APRIL 21

I confess, there are some days I don't much feel like praising. When disappointment or discouragement or heartache strikes, praise is the last thing on my mind or heart. But you know something? When I begin lifting His name, my dark mood lifts. My situation might not change, but my attitude does. This life throws lots of changes at us, but God never changes. He is always there, always faithful, always worthy of praise.

---

*Heavenly Father, in those moments
when life's challenges threaten to destroy my joy,
remind me that circumstances don't change who You are to me—
my Savior, Lord, and King. Let me ever praise You.*

Let us therefore come boldly unto the throne of grace, that we may obtain mercy, and find grace to help in time of need.
—Hebrews 4:16

APRIL 22

Have you ever been nervous about taking a problem or worry to someone because you were uncertain of their reaction? I'm sure we all have. But we never have to be nervous about approaching God. He already knows our deepest needs, thoughts, and concerns. He's ready to comfort us, advise us, guide us, and forgive us as soon as we ask. Isn't it wonderful to have such a loving Father?

Heavenly Father, thank You that I can always talk to You, sharing my fears, my worries, my heartaches, my joys, or my failings. You always listen and care. Thank You for Your grace.

LORD, lift thou up the light of thy countenance upon us.
—Psalm 4:6b

APRIL 23

Nobody likes being the dark. I'm speaking from a metaphorical sense. The phrase "being in the dark" can mean feeling foolish and insignificant. But when we stand in the light of God's grace, we realize how valuable we are in His eyes. When we ask Him to shine upon us, we're asking for His wisdom. No foolishness there!

Heavenly Father, thank You for Your light that enlightens and strengthens us.

He restoreth my soul: he leadeth me in the paths of righteousness for his name's sake.
—Psalm 23:3

APRIL 24

People often bemoan, "Why am I here? What is my purpose?" A Christian never has to ponder such a dismal thought. Your purpose in this world is to reflect your Savior. You're to be salt and light. God restores you, He leads you on righteous pathways, not only because He knows it's what is best for you, but because it's the best way for you "glow Jesus." You are a living, breathing, flesh and bone example of our living God. "Wear" Him well!

---

*Heavenly Father, thank You for entrusting me
with the awesome responsibility and privilege
of pointing others to Your Son.
May I shine well for You!*

*I said, Lord, be merciful unto me:
heal my soul;
for I have sinned against thee.*
—Psalm 41:4

APRIL 25

When we feel far from God, it isn't because He's gone anywhere. He is always faithful. Unfortunately, when we let sin run rampant in our lives, it pulls us away from Him. That separation is painful. The way to restore our relationship with Him is to confess that we've gone astray. He'll forgive the sin and wipe the slate clean, giving us the chance to straighten our steps. Merciful healing descends with a few simple words: "I'm sorry; please forgive me."

---

*Heavenly Father, please search me and rid me
of any sinfulness that distances me from You.
Let me draw closer to You day by day
as I serve You and practice Your ways.*

*My doctrine shall drop as the rain,
my speech shall distil as the dew,
as the small rain upon the tender herb,
and as the showers upon the grass:*
—Deuteronomy 32:2

APRIL 26

There's something so satisfying about breathing in the air after a refreshing rain. God's Word brings the same refreshing and renewal to our souls when we choose to follow His instructions. No life is too far gone to be made new again. Stand beneath the shower of His loving guidance and experience the renewal it can bring.

---

*Heavenly Father, thank You for being a Restorer.
Rain down Your mercy and grace on me today
and let me stand clean and blameless in Your presence.*

> Not that we are sufficient of ourselves to think any thing as of ourselves; but our sufficiency is of God;
> —2 Corinthians 3:5

APRIL 27

Have you ever felt too weak to stand? So often I've found myself floundering, insufficient, unable. But we don't have to move forward in our own strength. Our God is sufficient, and He endows us with His strength when ours is gone. We might be inadequate, but God is always more than adequate. He catches us when we fall and sets us on our feet again, able to stand secure because we're bolstered by His love.

---

*Heavenly Father, Your strength is perfect.
You are able to meet my every need.
Thank You for bolstering me and making me complete.*

*The Lord recompense thy work,
and a full reward be given thee
of the LORD God of Israel,
under whose wings
thou art come to trust.*
—Ruth 2:12

APRIL 28

There are positive and negative consequences to everything we do. But you know what? When we choose to trust God, there are only positive consequences. He grows us, works through us, lets us share His love with others, and gives us opportunities to be a blessing. Commit your way to Him—you'll never regret it.

*Heavenly Father, as I go about my day and duties,
may I remember You are present and mindful of me.
Bless the work of my hands.*

God, who is rich in mercy, for his great love wherewith he loved us, Even when we were dead in sins, hath quickened us together with Christ, (by grace ye are saved;)
—Ephesians 2:4-5

APRIL 29

I think most of us would agree God is better at unconditional loving than humans are. We like to practice the "you scratch my back, I'll scratch yours" kind of love. But God is bigger than that. He. Just. Loves. And because He loves us so mightily, we should want to live in a way that pleases Him. Not to earn His love, but to show our appreciation to Him. When we choose to live in a way His Word directs, not only do we make our Father happy, we can avoid the regrets and unpleasant consequences of wallowing in sin. There is great security in living within the bounds of God's loving arms.

Heavenly Father, thank You for loving me and making me an heir with Christ. May my life bear witness to the joy of my salvation.

*And they that know thy name
will put their trust in thee:
for thou, LORD, hast not forsaken them
that seek thee.*
—Psalm 9:10

APRIL 30

Until they're proven untrustworthy, a child instinctively trusts her parents to keep her safe, to love her, and to meet her needs. Unfortunately, many times parents fail and break that fragile bond of trust. But our Father-God has never and will never forsake His own. Do you need someone on whom to depend? Seek Him. He's waiting.

---

*Heavenly Father, thank You for being trustworthy
and always available to Your children.
Let my heart seek to stay in right relationship with You.*

Examine me, O Lord, and prove me; try my reins and my heart. For thy lovingkindness is before mine eyes: and I have walked in thy truth.
—Psalm 26:2-3

MAY 1

Wouldn't it be wonderful to stand faultless before God, having always lived in reliance on Him and in obedience to Him? What an impossible goal... Or is it?

You see, God judges our hearts. When we stumble (because we will) and we confess our shortcomings (because if the Holy Spirit is within us, we'll be convicted to do so), the sin is forgiven and wiped away as if it never existed at all. Our heart can be pure before Him. Isn't that awesome?

Heavenly Father, thank You for grace that covers my sins. May I never take advantage of Your grace but strive to daily walk in Your truth.

> **LORD, I have loved the habitation of thy house, and the place where thine honour dwelleth.**
> —Psalm 26:8

MAY 2

Have you heard the Mercy Me song "I Can Only Imagine"? This line always gets me: "Surrounded by Your glory, what will my heart feel? Will I dance for You, Jesus, or in awe of You be still?" The song is aptly titled because at this point we can only imagine. But one day, if you're a believer, you will be in Jesus' glorious presence. Such a beautiful promise for us—eternity in the place where His glory dwells.

Hold tight to His promises! Endless joy awaits us.

Heavenly Father, thank You for the promise of heaven and the glory that awaits me!

> But whoso keepeth his word, in him verily is the love of God perfected: hereby know we that we are in him. He that saith he abideth in him ought himself also so to walk, even as he walked.
> —1 John 2:5-6

MAY 3

I've always loved and respected my parents. When I was a child, I tried to be obedient not out of fear of punishment but because I didn't want to disappoint my mom and dad. Their opinion mattered.

As children of God, His opinion should matter more than any other. We show God we love and respect Him by keeping His commandments. If we say we're His children, then we have a standard to follow: Jesus' example. I can never be perfect, but I can be holy—set apart to do His will rather than seeking my own.

Walk as children of Light. There is such joy in being complete *in Him*.

Heavenly Father, I love You. I stand in awe of Your might and power. May I abide by Your precepts and please You in the way I walk this earth.

*And the Spirit and the bride say, Come.
And let him that heareth say, Come.
And let him that is athirst come.
And whosoever will,
let him take the water of life freely.*
—Revelation 22:17

MAY 4

The Holy Spirit whispers to lost sinners, "Come." Many ignore the plea and go on living separated from God. But for those who respond—those who turn at the call to come and accept Jesus as Savior and Lord—those souls are quenched with a deeply satisfying love, with joy and peace that defies explanation. The longer someone refuses the tug on their heart, the more hardened they become. How devastating this must be for the Father who longs for a relationship with each of His created. The Living Water is a gift free to all who choose to believe. Will you pray for all lost sinners to heed the call?

---

*Heavenly Father, thank You for Your saving grace
which is available to all.
Please continue to tap on the heart of those I know and love
who don't yet know You as Savior.
May Your will be done in their lives and mine.*

Wait on the LORD: be of good courage, and he shall strengthen thine heart: wait, I say, on the LORD.
—Psalm 27:14

MAY 5

Sometimes I think about the people who've gone before me and I want to be with them. Sometimes I look at the problems of this world and I long for God to call me Home. But you know what? There's a purpose for me on this earth, just as there is for you. God will reveal His goodness to us as we walk these earthly pathways. He will give us the strength to endure sadness or trials. We can wait in confidence for Him to call us to Him. Take heart, stand firm, and wait for the Lord—His time is always best.

Heavenly Father, thank You for the strength You give.
Thank You for the plans You make for each of Your children.
Let me use my time here wisely and store up treasures of eternal value.

> *And the world passeth away, and the lust thereof: but he that doeth the will of God abideth for ever.*
> —1 John 2:17

MAY 6

Some days I get so caught up in my agenda and the "right now" that I lose track of what is really important. Other days I squander, spending the minutes in useless pursuits. I need to remind myself that I'm given a certain number of days, and those days are meant to be spent seeking and doing God's will. That doesn't mean I have to do anything big and important every day, but serving my family with a happy heart, smiling at a stranger, offering a word of encouragement to a friend... These are little things that bring glory to the One who saved me. Are we storing up treasures in heaven by impacting the lives of those we encounter?

Heavenly Father, let me turn my ear to Your prompting, and let me achieve the tasks that will best bring glory to You.

...he that acknowledgeth the Son hath the Father also.
—1 John 2:23b

MAY 7

Lots of people talk about God. Sometimes in a flippant way, such as calling Him "the man upstairs" or "my higher power," which seems to diminish Him. I call this kind of treatment "giving a "nod" to God, and many act as if they believe a nod is enough.

But you know what? If we bypass Jesus, we don't really know the Father. No man comes to the Father except through the Son. The Bible tells us we must acknowledge that Jesus is God's Son, who came to this earth to save man from his sins. When we confess this belief, then Jesus acts as the Mediator between us and God. To have a true relationship with the Father, we must receive the Son.

Heavenly Father, thank You for sending Jesus to take the penalty of my sin and to be the bridge that gives me direct access to You. May I never take lightly who You are to me.

> Little children, let no man deceive you: he that doeth righteousness is righteous, even as he is righteous.
> —1 John 3:7

MAY 8

Remember the children's song, "Oh, be careful little feet where you go..."? There's so much truth in that warning. When I was in high school and preparing to go out with friends, my mom often reminded me that wherever I went, I took the Holy Spirit. She told me to ask myself if He would be comfortable where I was going. A few times this kept me from following through with plans.

Too easily we can follow a pathway that leads to destruction. Sometimes it's wise to stop, examine the surroundings, and ask yourself if this a place God would choose for you. If not, turn around! This world is full of temptations, but the Holy Spirit gives us the strength to stay the course when we set our hearts toward Him.

Heavenly Father, thank You for the guidance of Your Spirit, which resides within me.
Let me heed His instruction and remain on a righteous path.

> Marvel not, my brethren, if the world hate you.
> —1 John 3:13

MAY 9

Being popular is so important to many people. Everyone wants to be liked and accepted. But the thing is, as Christians, we won't be accepted by the world. Not if we're truly following Christ. The world's desires and Christ's desires are too often in opposition. We might have to face rejection or outright persecution for staying true to our Christian convictions, but believe me—it's worth the cost. Christ died for us; the least we can do is live for Him.

Heavenly Father, please give me the strength to stay true to my convictions and to show love to those who treat You like an enemy. May I win them to You with my steadfast love.

> *In whom we have redemption through his blood, the forgiveness of sins…*
> —Ephesians 1:7a

MAY 10

When I was a child and knew I'd done wrong, I avoided being in my parents' presence. Which was awful, because I loved my mom and dad. Sin is a terrible burden to carry. It weighs us down. It sags us with regret and self-recrimination and makes us desire to hide. But, praise God, we don't have to remain encumbered by our poor choices and wrong living—we can be redeemed. Jesus paid the price! Ask His forgiveness and step forward in freedom. Forgiveness is a beautiful gift.

Heavenly Father, thank You for forgiveness and the cleansing that comes with confession. May no sin interfere with my fellowship with You.

And let us not be weary in well doing: for in due season we shall reap, if we faint not.
—Galatians 6:9

MAY 11

Have you ever caught yourself thinking, "What's the use? I give up..." Doing right and good things isn't easy, and sometimes it might seem as though doing good earns us nothing more than ridicule or footprints up our spine. But who are we trying to please: people or our Lord?

On this earth we might never find the appreciation for which our heart yearns, but when we reach Heaven we will see the harvest our choices produced. Don't give up! Our reward waits on the side of eternity.

Heavenly Father, please guard me against a defeatist attitude. Strengthen me to serve You well, and may Your Son's name be glorified in my efforts.

> *Bear ye one another's burdens, and so fulfil the law of Christ.*
> —**Galatians 6:2**

MAY 12

Have you ever stopped and considered that Jesus, the Son of God, came to earth to *serve*? As God's Son, He could have commanded everyone to bow down and serve Him, but instead He served. If Christ—God's Son, our Savior and Lord—lowered Himself to carry others' burdens, should I then ignore a brother or sister in need? There are countless needs around us, and we can't meet all of them. But if we rely on the Holy Spirit's prompting, we will know to whom we should stretch out a hand of assistance. And we can always lift others in our prayers.

Jesus claimed the least would be first in His kingdom. Being "least" doesn't come naturally, but for Christians, it is an expectation.

---

*Heavenly Father, open my heart to those You want me to serve.
Let me love as You loved and give as You give
so souls might be won to Your kingdom.*

*He restoreth my soul:
he leadeth me in the paths of
righteousness for his name's sake.*
—Psalm 23:3

MAY 13

When my middle daughter was a little girl, she had a tendency to wander off in public places. Mostly because she'd start chatting with someone and forget she was supposed to be with us. Whether it was Walmart, the flea market, or an amusement park, when we realized she wasn't with us anymore, we immediately went on a search for her. Thank the Lord, He always kept her safe, and she eventually outgrew her penchant for wandering.

If a sheep falls away from the flock, a loving shepherd doesn't leave it lost and floundering. He seeks it out and restores it to its position as part of the flock. Jesus does the same for us. When we wander away, His Spirit pursues us, prompting us to return. When we do return, Jesus forgives us and restores us to fellowship with God. Once we're in right fellowship again, we are deeply satisfied and complete.

---

*Heavenly Father, thank You for loving me enough to pursue me.
May I remain in Your "flock" and find my contentment
in You and You alone.*

> *What doth it profit, my brethren, though a man say he hath faith, and have not works?*
> —James 2:14

MAY 14

One of my favorite parts of Sunday morning service is the children's feature. Kids are always so open and honest, and you never know what one of them might say in response to a question. One Sunday when my Bugaboos were in early grade school, the leader talked about love. She told the kids love isn't a smoochie, ooey feeling but is acts of kindness. Big Bugaboo raised his hand and said, "So, what you're saying is, 'love' is a verb." He definitely got it!

You know what? Faith is a verb, too. If we call ourselves Christians, then our actions and attitudes should reflect the truth. The world needs to *see* love in action. Don't just say, "I am a Christian"; be Christ-like in your behavior. That's faith in action.

---

*Heavenly Father, please give me a heart of service
and a desire to perform acts of love
that demonstrate my faith in You.*

Continue in prayer...
—Colossians 4:2a

MAY 15

Someone once asked me, "What's the point in praying if God's going to do what God's going to do regardless of what I say?" It's true that God does what God deems best. So do I, to the best of my limited human ability, as a mom and gramma, but that doesn't mean I don't want my kids or grandkids to talk to me. Relationships flounder when the parties cease to communicate.

Speaking to God is so very important for our relationship with Him. Talking to Him puts Him central in our thoughts. Prayer gives us a shield against the enemy. Satan's darts can't reach us when we're surrounded by God's presence, and we invite His presence through prayer. The point of prayer is to keep us in communion with the Father, which is the best place for us to be. Talk to your Father in heaven. He hears us when we call.

*Heavenly Father, thank You for listening when I pray.
Let my words to You serve to strengthen our bonds
and grow me in faith and trust.*

> For as the body without the spirit is dead, so faith without works is dead also.
> —James 2:26

MAY 16

Once the spirit leaves the body, our frame becomes a shell incapable of movement, speech, or breath. A person who proclaims Jesus as Lord but doesn't live out his faith is like a dead shell. When the Father looks at me, I want Him to see *breath*.

I'll never forget a walk to school with my dad the one winter we lived in Minnesota. The air was frigid but still, and every exhale created a little puff of condensation that hung like a miniature cloud in front of my face. Each breath was clearly visible. When He looks at us, does He see behaviors that reflect the Son? I pray so. How this world needs a glimpse of Jesus!

Heavenly Father, work in and through me so I give a glimpse of You in the things that I say and do.
Let me share the breath of life that only comes from Jesus.

If any man offend not in word, the same is a perfect man, and able also to bridle the whole body.
—James 3:2b

MAY 17

Once words are out there, you can't take them back. Words hold power to invite or alienate, to encourage or crush, to build up or break down. I have such admiration for people who speak the truth in love and then back up their statements with consistent, faithful action. The person who keeps his promises, who speaks words of affirmation, and who refuses to wallow in ugliness or indecency truly is a person of integrity and maturity. Such a person is a reflection of our Lord Jesus.

Heavenly Father, give me control of my tongue so the words I speak bring glory to You.

> *And I will remember my covenant, which is between me and you and every living creature of all flesh; and the waters shall no more become a flood to destroy all flesh.*
> —Genesis 9:15

MAY 18

I love this promise from God. I think of this and all His other promises each time I see a rainbow in the sky. I also think of this promise in the middle of a storm—whether an actual weather-related storm or a personal, emotional storm. God will never send so much rain that it covers the earth; God will never allow so much difficulty that it collapses me emotionally. His presence sustains. His promises give hope. His love overwhelms. I'm so glad I'm His, and He is mine!

---

*Heavenly Father, thank You for the covenant
that binds me to You eternally.
Let me trust in Your promises and walk in confidence,
bolstered by Your strength.*

Jesus answered and said unto her, Whosoever drinketh of this water shall thirst again: But whosoever drinketh of the water that I shall give him shall never thirst; but the water that I shall give him shall be in him a well of water springing up into everlasting life.
—John 4:13-14

MAY 19

When you are really, really thirsty—dry and parched and on the verge of dehydration—there is only one drink that will quench you: water. Nothing else, no matter how colorful (juice) or bubbly (soda) or aromatic (coffee) satisfies. Only water.

Guess what? The same is true of our souls. We can try to fill ourselves with the attractive, tempting, exciting things of the world, but we will always experience a dissatisfaction in the center of our hearts until we've been filled with the love of Jesus. He is the Living Water that meets our deepest need and completes as nothing else can. Drink of Him and His love today and be filled to overflowing!

---

*Heavenly Father, thank You for Your Son
who entered this world to bridge the gap between God and man.
Thank You for the satisfaction and fulfillment that comes
from a relationship with You through Him.
Thank You for filling me up with Your love.*

One thing have I desired of the Lord, that will I seek after; that I may dwell in the house of the Lord all the days of my life…
—Psalm 27:4

MAY 20

Let's face it, this earth offers some beautiful sights. God placed us in a world with waterfalls and rainbows, towering trees and flowers of every imaginable shape and color. The beauty of the world is a gift to us from Him, and we should give it good care and take the time to appreciate its grandeur. But what we see down here pales in comparison to what waits for us in heaven. I'm so grateful Jesus went to prepare a place for those who love Him and live to serve Him. There's unspeakable peace in knowing I have an eternal Home in His presence.

Heavenly Father, thank You for the dwelling place waiting for me. While I wait to inhabit it, let me serve You openly and wholeheartedly.

For the Lamb which is in the midst of the throne shall feed them, and shall lead them unto living fountains of waters: and God shall wipe away all tears from their eyes.
—Revelation 7:17

MAY 21

I'm not in any hurry to die—I have a lot to live for, including the six Sweeties, two Bugaboos, and pair of Wugmumps who call me Gramma. *smile* But at the same time I'm eager for the day when God will wipe away my tears (no more crying there!) and I will meet my Savior face to face.

While I'm still on this earth, my daily prayer is that my children and my grandchildren and the generations to come will know Jesus intimately and live to serve Him. My heart aches with the desire for each of them to know the joy of the Lord while they walk this earth and then be with me and those faithful saints who've gone before us in Heaven, the place where sorrow and pain and sin is never found. I can think of no greater blessing than to know my children and grandchildren's souls are secure. Thank the Lord for the assurance of salvation!

Heavenly Father, Your salvation lasts into eternity.
May my children, grandchildren,
and all the generations to come know the joy
of walking in right relationship with You.

> *And I will walk at liberty:*
> *for I seek thy precepts.*
> —Psalm 119:45

MAY 22

Our country has laws which its citizens are expected to follow. If we break those laws, we can expect to be prosecuted and punished for our crime. Sometimes that punishment includes spending time in prison. But when we obey the rules of the country, we enjoy freedom.

Freedom from the penalties of law is nice, but freedom from the penalty of sin is much greater. When we follow God's guidance—His precepts—we can enjoy freedom the burdens of guilt and regret and self-recrimination. Sometimes our own personal "jail cells" are worse than anything the law could inflict upon us. Jesus came to give freedom from sin's snare. Follow His will for your life and enjoy freedom.

Heavenly Father, thank You for saving me from the penalty of death.
May I follow Your guidance so my path is straight
and free from sin's snares.

Stand fast therefore in the liberty wherewith Christ hath made us free, and be not entangled again with the yoke of bondage.
—Galatians 5:1

MAY 23

*J*have a dear friend who often includes in her prayers thankfulness to God for freeing her from addictions. She understands too well the heartache of being bound to something harmful, and she appreciates the strength God gave her to break those chains.

There are so many chains that can bind us: chains of alcoholism, drug abuse, gambling, immoral behavior... If we've accepted Jesus as Lord, those behaviors that steal our attention from and affection for doing His will are cumbersome burdens indeed. Jesus didn't save us to let us wallow in destructive acts; He saved us to live free from sin's yoke of slavery. Whatever battle you're fighting, Jesus holds the victory and He wants to give it to you. But you have to lay the burden at His feet...and leave it there.

Heavenly Father, if there are habits that keep from freely serving You and glorifying You with my behavior, rid me of them. Fill me so thoroughly with Your Spirit that there isn't room for any harmful thing of this world.

For, brethren, ye have been called unto liberty; only use not liberty for an occasion to the flesh, but by love serve one another.
—Galatians 5:13

MAY 24

There's a verse in the sixth chapter of I Corinthians that says we have the right to do anything, but not everything is beneficial to us. I used to tell my fifth graders that rights should never be confused with responsibilities. As mature believers, we have a responsibility toward our new brothers and sisters in the Lord to provide them with examples that won't lead them astray. We have a responsibility to ourselves to not engage in behavior that might bring destruction to our relationship with Christ. If we harbor a servant heart rather than a selfish heart, we'll likely make the right choices for ourselves and our fellow believers. Perhaps a rule of comma usage applies here: When in doubt, leave it out!

Heavenly Father, thank You for liberty!
Please help me live in a way that sets a good example
to "younger" believers and edifies the body as a whole.

Nevertheless when it shall turn to the Lord, the vail shall be taken away. Now the Lord is that Spirit: and where the Spirit of the Lord is, there is liberty. But we all, with open face beholding as in a glass the glory of the Lord, are changed into the same image from glory to glory, even as by the Spirit of the Lord.
—Colossians 3:16-18

MAY 25

One of the first projects I completed in calligraphy way back during my high school days was this phrase: "In the world of science, one must experience to believe; in the world of Jesus, one must believe to experience." That is so true! When we ask Jesus in faith to be our Savior, the veil is taken away. We see sin for what it is—an ugly robber of joy and peace. We see the love that led Jesus to the cross, and we develop a desire to live in a way that brings Him glory. A Christian is meant to be a "little Christ"—a reflection of Him. Shine for Jesus, my friend!

---

*Heavenly Father, thank You for growing me
in wisdom and discernment.
Please expand my faith and give me opportunities
to share the truth of Your love with those around me.*

Lord, thou hast been our dwelling place in all generations. Before the mountains were brought forth, or ever thou hadst formed the earth and the world, even from everlasting to everlasting, thou art God.
—Psalm 90:1-2

MAY 26

I have the joy and privilege of having come from a long line of faithful saints. Even though I never met my maternal grandparents or great-grandparents, I know from the stories my mother shared that my ancestors loved and served the Lord. The same Father-God to whom my great-grandfathers prayed is the same Father-God my little Wugmumps address in their nighttime prayers. He was, He is, and He always will be from everlasting to everlasting. Nothing else gives us a guarantee of forever except God. If that knowledge doesn't wash you in a warm flow of security, I don't know what will.

Heavenly Father, thank You for being my dwelling place.
I pray for every member of my family, both those living now
and those to come, to receive Your Son as Savior
and to serve You with their whole hearts.
May every generation rise up and call You blessed.

For a thousand years in thy sight are but as yesterday when it is past, and as a watch in the night.
—Psalm 90:4

MAY 27

We humans tend to measure everything by time. (Some drivers seem to think if they arrive at a place a minute ahead of everyone else, they've accomplished something spectacular.) The older I get, the faster time seems to go—and I'm not referencing MPH! But time has a different meaning when you put it in terms of eternity.

I lost my mom in November of 2018. After her death, I dreamed I encountered her (in an antique store, of all places) and rushed to hug her. "Mom, it's so good to see you! It's been so long!" She said, "Yes, it's been a thousand years." I corrected her: "No, Mom, only a few weeks." And she said with a smile I'll never forget, "No, it's been a thousand wonderful years."

Right now I can't imagine a thousand years in heaven, but someday it will be a reality for all of us who believe. So many mysteries...and they'll be made clear when we reach the place of glory.

Heavenly Father, thank You for heaven where Your saints will reside eternally and where all uncertainties will be made known.

So teach us to number our days, that we may apply our hearts unto wisdom.
—Psalm 90:12

MAY 28

Have you ever noticed on old headstones the way the deceased's life is recorded? They would carve the number of years, months, and days the person spent on the earth, counting each day as significant. I've wondered if they were inspired by this particular scripture.

We all have a limited number of days on this earth. I don't want to waste my time here, but sometimes time gets away from me. Some evenings I look back at the day and wonder if I accomplished anything of value. A wise person values each hour, recognizing that it will never come again. Am I using my time for good purposes? Am I building pleasant memories? Am I leaving something of value behind? And—best question of all—am I spending time with my Father each day? Time with Him certainly builds a heart a of wisdom.

---

*Heavenly Father, time is fleeting, each moment precious.
Let me be a good steward of my hours
so I need not carry any regret about time wasted.*

And let the beauty of the Lord our God be upon us: and establish thou the work of our hands upon us; yea, the work of our hands establish thou it.
—**Psalm 90:17**

MAY 29

I'm sure you've heard the phrase, "Idle hands are the devil's workshop." I read a report about three young teens who broke into a store and ransacked the place. When asked why they'd done it, one said, "We didn't have anything else to do."

No one likes to be overtaxed, but nothing to do sometimes leads us to activities we wouldn't define as wise. When we ask God to help us make good use of our time, He will guide us in the best activities for our hands. God gives the blessing of work, of accomplishing good for His glory and our wellbeing. When our work, activities, and efforts are done with the purpose of honoring His Kingdom, then His favor rests on us and our endeavors will have positive eternal value.

---

*Heavenly Father, thank You for work and the benefit it serves.
Let me use my hands for good and not evil,
and may my attitude toward service reflect the heart of Your Son.*

In every thing give thanks: for this is the will of God in Christ Jesus concerning you.
—1 Thessalonians 5:18

MAY 30

Every now and then, as a conversation starter, I'll ask one of my grandkids, "What are you thankful for?" Not once have any of them said they're thankful for a hardship. But this scripture declares we're to be grateful in all things...even the hard things of life. And you know what? It's a sound idea.

When I look back at my life, the trials are what made me stronger, that solidified my trust and dependence on God. How can I begrudge something that drew me closer to Him? It isn't easy to be thankful for the ash pile, but we can be thankful for the One who doesn't leave us there alone and who can bring good out of every life situation.

Thankfulness might not change the situation, but it changes us. Maybe that's why it's God's will for us to be thankful in all circumstances.

---

*Heavenly Father, please give me a heart of gratitude
that results in a positive attitude
regardless of life's circumstances.*

> As ye have therefore received Christ Jesus the Lord, so walk ye in him: Rooted and built up in him, and stablished in the faith, as ye have been taught, abounding therein with thanksgiving.
> —Colossians 2:6-7

MAY 31

We have a quartet of cats. Every morning I fill their food bowls—two medium sized bowls and two larger ones. I put the exact same amount of food in each bowl, but because two of the bowls are smaller, the food heaps up and spills over. These are the bowls to which the cats gravitate—the overflowing ones.

There's something appealing about overflowing. As Christians, we are to abound therein—overflow—with thankfulness. Some days might seem bleak and wrought with conflict, but we still have reason for thankfulness. Jesus saved us! No circumstance changes who He was, is, and always will be—your Savior and Lord. When you're glum, remember whose you are, and let your heart well up in gratitude for the One who will never leave us nor forsake us.

*Heavenly Father, thank You that no circumstance—
not even death—can rob me of my place as Your child.
May my heart be ever mindful and appreciative
of Your presence in my life.*

Thou believest that there is one God; thou doest well: the devils also believe, and tremble.
—James 2:19

JUNE 1

So many people think they're okay because they believe "in God." James was pretty blunt about it: even demons believe, and they shudder. There's a monumental difference between head knowledge and heart knowledge. Head knowledge is accepting something as fact; heart knowledge is being dedicated to its truth. For instance, we can say we know it's smart to exercise every day, but dedication puts us on the treadmill every morning.

It isn't enough to believe in God. One must believe in his heart on the Lord Jesus Christ, must confess with his lips that Jesus is Lord, and must ask Him to be one's Savior. On the day of judgment there will be countless people turned away from Heaven because they only believed "in God." Have you taken the steps to know Jesus and become a child of God?

Heavenly Father, may my relationship with You be more than head knowledge. Consume my heart so I may fully reside in Your grace.

> *Wherefore we receiving a kingdom which cannot be moved, let us have grace, whereby we may serve God acceptably with reverence and godly fear:*
> —Hebrews 12:28

JUNE 2

Have you read the end of Bible? If yes, then you know what is to come. No matter what it might look like on this earth, Jesus already holds the victory! He has overcome every evil and will reign forever. God's kingdom cannot be shaken. There will be a judgment day, and we're wise to consider that day with reverential fear. However, for the redeemed, there is no fear of condemnation. Is that not reason to shout out thankfulness to God? Let's give Him the gratitude He deserves for preparing such an amazing eternal plan for those of us who believe!

Heavenly Father, my future is secure because I am Your child. Let me stand strong and confident in the face of the world's conflicts, resting in the assurance that You are Victor over evil.

*Since we heard of your faith in Christ Jesus,
and of the love which ye have to all the saints,
For the hope which is laid up for you in heaven...*
—Colossians 1:4-5a

JUNE 3

A day of judgment will arrive, a day when each of us will answer for the decisions we've made. The most important question we must answer will be, "Did You know My Son?" Those of us who have accepted Jesus as Savior and Lord will enter heaven's gates with rejoicing; those who rejected the Son will suffer God's eternal wrath.

None of us know when that day will be, but we need to be ready. We need to commit ourselves to Him and then live in a way that guides others to the knowledge of His grace. If you've been justified and saved, don't keep Him to yourself. Spread the Good News!

---

*Heavenly Father, let my love for You spill over
in words of truth that guide the lost to the saving grace
You alone can give.*

...desire that ye might be filled with the knowledge of his will in all wisdom and spiritual understanding; That ye might walk worthy of the Lord unto all pleasing, being fruitful in every good work, and increasing in the knowledge of God;
—Colossians 1:9b-10

JUNE 4

It is getting harder and harder to openly live our faith in this country that was founded on Godly principles. It makes my heart sad to see Jesus's name being trampled, prayers being squashed, and God being chased from all public places. You and I may well be the only example of Christ the people around us encounter. Therefore it is imperative for us to grow in spiritual understanding, to walk in a way that points others to Him. Go forth and bear fruit! Please Him with your words and actions! Seek His will and follow it! Oh, how people need to see Jesus in you.

Heavenly Father, let me live in such a way that people who don't know You will want to know You because they see You in me.

*He giveth power to the faint;
and to them that have no might
he increaseth strength.*
—Isaiah 40:29

JUNE 5

There's a funny thing about conflicts–they don't seem to come one at a time. Sometimes life's trials overwhelm us and we quaver beneath the weight of conflict and heartache. But this I have learned: When I am weak, I can lean into Him and He will sustain me. Children sing, "God is bigger than the bogeyman..." The song is cute and whimsical, but the lyrics are also true. There is no power on earth that compares to the power of the Creator of heaven and earth. What does that mean? This truth: I am never powerless because I am His.

---

*Heavenly Father, when life crashes in, it's easy to want to crumble.
Help me stand strong in the power of Your presence.
Use life's trials to build my spiritual muscles,
and let me an example of faith under fire.*

> In whom ye also trusted,
> after that ye heard the word of truth,
> the gospel of your salvation:
> in whom also after that ye believed,
> ye were sealed
> with that holy Spirit of promise.
> —Ephesians 1:13

JUNE 6

Lots of times the Holy Spirit gets overlooked in the Trinity, but what an important role He plays in our lives. He is our seal of salvation. He is our constant companion, helper, and guide. He is God's very Spirit residing within us. I was a bashful little girl who moved frequently, always the new kid in class, and sometimes I felt very alone. But when I accepted Jesus as my Savior, my "alone" status changed. Wherever I went, the Holy Spirit was with me, and even as a child I found comfort in that realization. Dear Christian, don't be lonely, for you are never alone.

Heavenly Father, in moments when I feel as if no one is there or no one cares, remind me that Your Spirit is ever with me. In You let me find my peace and contentment.

> *O lord, thou hast searched me, and known me.*
> —Psalm 139:1

JUNE 7

Sometimes people don't "get" us. They misunderstand the meaning of our words, they misinterpret the motives of our actions, or they misread our expressions or body language and draw incorrect conclusions. Other times we can fool people into believing something incorrect about us. But God knows us inside and out. He crafted us in our mother's womb! No one understands us and loves us as unconditionally as God our Father. If you're feeling misunderstood and under-appreciated, look up—God knows.

---

*Heavenly Father, thank You for truly seeing me,
every part of me, and loving me so deeply.
Thank You for knowing what I need and being willing
to meet those needs. I am complete because of You.*

Thou hast beset me behind and before, and laid thine hand upon me.
—Psalm 139:5

JUNE 8

The concept that God is always there can be hard to grasp. I remember lying in bed as a little girl, trying to wrap my mind around the idea that God has no beginning and end, but as confusing as it might be, it's also comforting. God was with me every step in my past. He already waits around tomorrow's bend. No matter what I face today or what I will encounter tomorrow, He is there ready to arm me with strength and peace and comfort. His hand bolsters me with every breath I take. What a loving, attentive Father He is.

Heavenly Father, thank You for being the constant in my life. My security is ever in You.

> *Whither shall I go from thy spirit? or whither shall I flee from thy presence?*
> —Psalm 139:7

JUNE 9

When I was in junior high, my mother and I went to a softball game in another town. As we were leaving the game, a horrible storm blew in. Thick rolling clouds brought rain so thick and heavy the entire landscape was black. We couldn't see even a few inches of the road to be able to drive. So we sat in the car while wind, rain, and hail pummeled the vehicle. I really wanted my dad, but he didn't know where we were and, even if he had, he could have driven right past us without realizing it.

Guess what? That never happens with God. His Spirit resides within us, so we're never without His presence. Elsewhere in Psalm 139 it says that even the night is like day to Him. There is no where that we aren't under His watchful attention.

---

*Heavenly Father, You promised to never leave me,
and You keep Your promises.
Thank You for the assurance I have with You.*

> *For thou hast possessed my reins:*
> *thou hast covered me in my mother's womb.*
> *I will praise thee; for I am fearfully*
> *and wonderfully made: marvelous are thy works;*
> *and that my soul knoweth right well.*
> —Psalm 139:13-14

JUNE 10

I have a tendency to be too hard on myself, and I spent too many years worrying about not being good enough. But you know what? God created me with brownish-blonde hair and blue-gray eyes and a lack of athletic prowess. He knit me together in my mother's womb, and who am I to question God's hand of creation? He gave me *life*, and as His child my focus should be living to glorify to Him rather than living to please myself or impress humans (who will never love me the way He loves).

You are wonderfully made by the Creator of the universe who breathed His breath into your lungs! He never looks at you and wonders "How did *that* happen?" No, He looks at You and thinks, "My beloved child." When you're feeling glum, say these words: "God loves me and that's more than good enough."

Heavenly Father, thank You for giving me life and purpose.
I am loved by You, and Your love is my Enough.

...in thy book all my members were written, which in continuance were fashioned, when as yet there was none of them.
—Psalm 139:16b

JUNE 11

Even before you were born, God knew you. He had a glorious plan for your life that would bring you joy and satisfaction. We can get off course, and sometimes when things are really tough we even consider bringing our lives to a premature end. But don't you follow through on that kind of thinking! God is the giver of life. He determines how many breaths we take. If we cut His plan short, we miss out on the blessings He has planned for us. Trust your life to the Maker of the heavens and earth. He knows best.

---

*Heavenly Father, thank You for giving me life.
Help me live it to the abundance You have planned for me.*

> *I exhort therefore, that, first of all, supplications, prayers, intercessions, and giving of thanks, be made for all men; For kings, and for all that are in authority; that we may lead a quiet and peaceable life in all godliness and honesty.*
> —1 Timothy 2:1-2

JUNE 12

I am grateful to live in America. My great-grandparents left Russia in 1874 in search of religious freedom being denied them by the Russian czar, and they found it here. No country on this earth is perfect, but we have more freedom than any other country in the world. We should appreciate these freedoms but never take them for granted. God's admonition for us to pray for those in authority is one we are wise to take to heart. Our leaders need God's wisdom and discernment as they make decisions that will impact us for years to come.

Heavenly Father, You place leaders into positions of authority. Please grant them Your wisdom and help them make decisions that will benefit this country.
May we always be able to say that God blesses America.

> *For this is good and acceptable in the sight of God our Saviour; Who will have all men to be saved, and to come unto the knowledge of the truth.*
> —1 Timothy 2:3-4

JUNE 13

How the Father wants to call every person His child. It is His will that none should perish. All of us know and love people who are destined for eternal separation from God. I have one friend who often prays, "God, please let everyone find salvation." Her prayer, offered from a tender heart, humbles me. I tend to pray for those I know personally, but more and more God reminds me I need to "broaden my scope" and pray for those outside of my small circle of acquaintance. Will you join me in praying salvation for all? What a different world this would be if all honored God and called Him Father.

---

*Heavenly Father, You love every soul born
and You desire a relationship with every person.
Open the hearts of the lost to You and make Your Son known to them.
Father, draw the lost from darkness into Your Light of eternity.*

For there is one God, and one mediator between God and men, the man Christ Jesus;
—1 Timothy 2:5

JUNE 14

Jesus has lot of roles—Savior, Redeemer, Example... But Mediator is also important. There are times when I'm so burdened, so worn down, so clueless as to what would be best, I don't know what or how to pray. I can trust in those times, that when I open my heart, Jesus interprets all the pain, weariness, and confusion, and then communicates it to the Father. Jesus stands in front of me, so when God looks at me, He sees the perfection of His Son instead of my broken state. Without Jesus, we can't reach the Father. I am so grateful He came, gave His life for lost sinners, rose triumphant over death, and now resides at His Father's side.

Heavenly Father, thank You for Jesus.

> *Even so must their wives be grave, not slanderers, sober, faithful in all things.*
> —1 Timothy 3:11

JUNE 15

Not to pick on us ladies, but some women have a reputation for being, well, catty. Others seem to relish passing on a juicy piece of gossip. The problem with cattiness or being gossipy is that it drives a wedge in relationships. We don't trust someone who has been condescending or has spoken ill of us.

It can be hard to hold our tongues, but when we do, we prove ourselves trustworthy and we better reflect the One who created us.

---

*Heavenly Father, please guard my reputation.
Let me speak and behave in ways that reflect You.*

For bodily exercise profiteth little: but godliness is profitable unto all things, having promise of the life that now is, and of that which is to come.
—1 Timothy 4:8

JUNE 16

My oldest daughter and her husband are very health conscious. My brother, his sons, and my youngest daughter run marathons and work out in preparation for the races. It's important to take care of our physical bodies, but no matter how much we exercise or what kind of healthy foods we eat, eventually our physical body will die. Our bodies are meant to break down. Not so for our spirits.

Being godly, being holy, has a purpose. It lets us point others to the Father. And more than that, it prepares us for eternity. I look forward to Heaven, to being with the faithful saints who have gone before me. I pray that my crown will be laden with jewels—not so I can boast, but so I have something of value to lay at Jesus' feet in appreciation for the sacrifice He made for me.

Heavenly Father, let me not neglect growing in grace and godliness. Let my life be spent furthering Your kingdom.

Who hath saved us, and called us with an holy calling, not according to our works, but according to his own purpose and grace, which was given us in Christ Jesus before the world began.
—1 Timothy 1:9

JUNE 17

A lot of people are confused about what it means to be a Christian. They expect Christians to be perfect. Um, can't be done (and boy, do I know it!). But we can be holy–set apart. God's grace has given us holiness. Living holy means making choices that glorify God rather than self. Living holy means speaking words of encouragement and edification rather than denigrating others or using foul talk. Living holy means reflecting the One who gave His life for us. We can't do it on our own–there is no one holy without Him–but, praise God, we can do it with His help! Let the world see Him in you. How the world needs our Savior.

---

*Heavenly Father, You knew I would be Yours
from the beginning of time.
Thank You for loving me even in my imperfections.
Grow me in discernment so I might better glorify You.*

> *For God hath not given us the spirit of fear; but of power, and of love, and of a sound mind.*
> —2 Timothy 1:7

JUNE 18

I admire people who stand up for their faith even to the point of arrest or persecution or death. Sometimes I wonder, if faced with the threat of physical harm or imprisonment, would I have the courage to remain strong? This verse gives the answer. When we depend on our own feeble strength, we will likely fall. But if we depend on His strength, we cannot fall.

It's so important for us to cultivate a relationship with the Father. If we are tapped into His Word and have built our spiritual muscles with prayer and communion with Him, on the day our faith is put to the test, our timidity will flee. His power will give us what we need. Prepare, dear Christian, for your day of battle, and trust Him to bring you to victory.

Heavenly Father, You arm me with courage and strength. May I be steadfast in faith and be a witness to Your power on the days of testing.

Who hath saved us, and called us with an holy calling, not according to our works, but according to his own purpose and grace, which was given us in Christ Jesus before the world began, But is now made manifest by the appearing of our Saviour Jesus Christ, who hath abolished death, and hath brought life and immortality to light through the gospel:
—2 Timothy 1:9-10

JUNE 19

When I was a little girl, the thought of death scared me so badly. I didn't want to die. Now I'm grown up, and I can't honestly say that I want to die (I have lots of things to live for!), but the idea of of dying no longer frightens me. I know where I'm going. I know Who is waiting for me with open arms. On the day I leave my earthly shell, I will see my Savior face to face. Jesus destroyed death! Tears sting as I consider that glorious moment of thanking Jesus personally for redeeming me and loving me in spite of my many failings.

Eternity awaits those who believe! God planned the means of accessing Heaven—through the grace of Jesus Christ—from before time began. Death isn't to be feared by the believer. In God's perfect timing for us, we will see our Father and we will live with Him forever and ever and ever. That is a cause for celebration.

Heavenly Father, because of Your Son, death has lost its sting. Thank You for welcoming me home someday.

Study to shew thyself approved unto God, a workman that needeth not to be ashamed, rightly dividing the word of truth.
—2 Timothy 2:15

JUNE 20

"... Rightly dividing [correctly handling] the word of truth." There are those who distort His Word, who twist it to serve their own purposes. So how can we know whether what we are hearing and speaking is truth? We need to be familiar with God's Word. (Counterfeit money experts can recognize a fake bill because they studiously examine real ones.) Spend time in the Bible. Read it. Study it. Memorize it. Hide its words in your heart so, when they're needed, they're available. Don't trust someone else's interpretation—seek confirmation for yourself. Ask the Holy Spirit to guide your heart and mind. The enemy wants to destroy, and he's able to manipulate those who skim the surface of God's Holy Word. So dig deep, and ask daily for God's wisdom. He grants wisdom to those who seek it.

Heavenly Father, gird me with truth so I walk uprightly and set an example of integrity for those I encounter.

> *I have gone astray like a lost sheep;*
> *seek thy servant; for I do not forget*
> *thy commandments.*
> —Psalm 119:176

JUNE 21

Several years ago, I saw a news story about a sheep that wandered away from its shepherd and got lost. Its wool grew so thick and heavy, the coat threatened his life! The sheep couldn't see. The weight of the coat made it almost impossible for him to move. (Story here: cnn.com/2015/09/03/asia/sheep-record-wool-shearer)

I saw so much truth in that story for us. When we wander away from our Shepherd we become weighted down. We become blinded to what is good and healthy and pure. But when we return to our Shepherd our lives are restored. If you feel mired down by poor choices, ask Jesus to rescue you. Like a loving shepherd seeks and saves his lost sheep, He will honor your prayer and welcome you into fellowship.

Heavenly Father, thank You for seeking me when I was lost.
Please bind my heart to You so I don't wander onto sinful pathways.

> *As newborn babes, desire the sincere milk of the word, that ye may grow thereby: If so be ye have tasted that the Lord is gracious.*
> —1 Peter 2:2-3

JUNE 22

There are things parents do to help their children grow up healthy: teach them to eat the right kinds of foods, to exercise, and to get enough rest. The Christian parent teaches their children to grow up healthy spiritually by taking them to church, reading Bible stories to them, and praying with them. Christian parents want their children to know that the Lord is good. If children develop their appetite for things of the Spirit, they'll learn to be satisfied by things that are so much better than anything the world offers. The best way to teach is by example. Moms and dads, grandmas and grandpas, are you craving spiritual milk and growing in your faith? Little eyes are watching.

Heavenly Father, let me set an example
of faithfulness others can emulate.
May I point to You in my words, actions, and attitude.

Having your conversation honest among the Gentiles: that, whereas they speak against you as evildoers, they may by your good works, which they shall behold, glorify God in the day of visitation.
—1 Peter 2:1-2

JUNE 23

Every now and then a pic pops up on Facebook that asks, "If you were arrested for being a Christian, would there be enough evidence to convict you?" It always makes me think...am I living what I believe? Wallowing in the world's practices severely damages our Christian witness.

A good litmus test for our activities is to ponder whether we'd be comfortable participating with Jesus sitting next to us. So many of the things that are acceptable by the world's standards are in direct conflict with the Holy Spirit. Why create such a battle inside ourselves?

Heavenly Father, please help me live in such a way that I would receive a unanimous guilty verdict on the charge of "glorifying God."

As free, and not using your liberty for a cloak of maliciousness, but as the servants of God.
—1 Peter 2:16

JUNE 24

I used to be guilty of saying, almost as a defense mechanism, "So I fouled up. God still loves me." Yes, He absolutely does love us. Nothing we do will ever change that. But as much as I love my children, when they do something wrong without any regard for what I've instructed or for how it will affect those who love them, it hurts my heart.

God's love is so much bigger than mine, so His hurt must be bigger, too, when His children deliberately stray into sin with the mindset that it doesn't matter because God will still love them. We are covered by grace, but we should never use God's grace as an excuse to do whatever we want to. God gave us boundaries to keep us safe and to help us live without regret and painful consequences. Enjoy freedom from the regret caused by past sins, but please don't take advantage of His grace.

*Heavenly Father, You sacrificed Your own Son
so I could know salvation.
Please help me conduct myself in a way
that shows my appreciation for the gift of grace.*

Fear thou not; for I am with thee: be not dismayed; for I am thy God: I will strengthen thee; yea, I will help thee; yea, I will uphold thee with the right hand of my righteousness.
—Isaiah 41:10

JUNE 25

Do you get uptight when you open the newspaper or turn on the TV? There are so many bad things happening both in the U.S. and in other countries. Sometimes I wonder what kind of world my grandchildren will inherit if circumstances don't change. Whenever I find myself drifting into worry, I read Isaiah 41:10.

Regardless of what is happening around us, we do not face the conflict alone. God is with us. He will strengthen us. He will help us. He holds us with His right hand—His hand of honor! That gives us security and is a reminder of how much we are loved by Him. We need not fear the world's troubles as long as we hold to Him...and He holds to us.

Heavenly Father, thank You that I need not wallow in fear or worry as long as You are on Your throne. Thank You for upholding me.

And he saith unto them, Follow me...
—Matthew 4:19a

JUNE 26

There's something so bright and cheerful about sunflowers. I love how they lift their heads and follow the sun's pathway as the day progresses. There's a good lesson in there for us—striving to keep our eyes on the Son. The thing is, when we stay focused on Him, the darkness and troubles of this world seem to fade. We become more aware of our blessings and we bask in the refreshment of His presence. In those moments when we feel lost and alone, it isn't because God moved. We have a responsibility to seek Him again. Then, once more, we will find refreshment of spirit and peace in our hearts.

Heavenly Father, please keep my eyes on Your Son and my heart tuned to Your will.

*When thou passest through the waters,
I will be with thee; and through the rivers,
they shall not overflow thee:
when thou walkest through the fire,
thou shalt not be burned;
neither shall the flame kindle upon thee.*
—Isaiah 43:2

JUNE 27

There is not one place in the Bible that promises our lives will be free of conflict. (Believe me, I've hunted for it!) In every life, including the Christian's life, there will be times when waters try to capsize our boats or flames attempt to fry us to a crisp. The world hates believers, and it will try to drag you down. But when we rely on our Anchor—when we remember Jesus is by our side—we can face those waters and flames with the knowledge that He already holds the victory. We can stand secure on His strength. Say this out loud: *He will be with me.* Take heart in that message, dear Christian. You are not alone.

---

*Heavenly Father, thank You for Your presence
in every moment of my life.
Let me lean into Your strength
and trust You to guide me through the troubled waters.*

I, even I, am the Lord; and beside me there is no saviour.
—Isaiah 43:11

JUNE 28

*T**hank you Lord, for saving my soul; Thank you Lord, for making me whole...* Have you ever sung the chorus from the song written by Seth and Bessie Sykes? It was fairly common in the 1970's and 1980's. It's a very simple chorus, but it holds so much truth.

There is only one way to fill the emptiness of our souls: a relationship with Jesus Christ. He is our only Savior. He is our only Fulfiller. You see, the name Yahweh is "I Am"—He is confirming His existence and, even more personal, He's confirming His presence. When He indwells us, we are complete. If you're trying to fill yourself with anything other than Him, you'll always feel empty. He is Yahweh. There is no other way to completion but Him.

Heavenly Father, thank You for satisfying the longing of my soul.

> *Giving thanks always for all things unto God and the Father in the name of our Lord Jesus Christ*
> —Ephesians 5:20

JUNE 29

It's easy to thank God for our blessings. But hardship can be a blessing in disguise. Hardship strengthens us and gives us an opportunity to show the difference God makes in a person's life.

When I was in my early twenties and in a very hard place. I called my mom and asked, "If God loves me so much, why am I here?" She responded, "Perhaps He's giving you the opportunity to gain strength for what is to come." I didn't much like that idea (in fact, I hung up on her!), but now I see the truth of it. That difficult time taught me to lean into God's strength and to trust Him to be there when no one else was. That growing time prepared me for other challenges to come.

He wastes nothing in our lives, so give God thanks for everything—even the hard things—because they serve to work His perfect will in and through us.

Heavenly Father, I will choose to praise You in the storms of life, knowing that nothing is wasted in Your kingdom.

We shall not all sleep, but we shall all be changed, In a moment, in the twinkling of an eye, at the last trump: for the trumpet shall sound, and the dead shall be raised incorruptible, and we shall be changed.
—1 Corinthians 15:51b-52

JUNE 30

"...In the twinkling of an eye" we will be changed. How I look forward to the trumpet sound! Can you imagine the celebration in heaven? What joy awaits those who believe; what heartbreak awaits those who don't. As we're building our relationship closer and closer to our Heavenly Father, let's remember to pray for those who are lost and continue to share God's love. The time is drawing near!

---

*Heavenly Father, as I listen for the trumpet call,
let me use these hours on earth wisely,
ever mindful that others need to know You, too.*

Therefore, my beloved brethren, be ye steadfast, unmoveable, always abounding in the work of the Lord, forasmuch as ye know that your labour is not in vain in the Lord.
—1 Corinthians 15:58

JULY 1

My mom was a very quiet person. She never sought the spotlight. But she was a diligent worker and homemaker, a wonderfully supportive wife to my dad, and an attentive, dedicated mother to my brother and me. At the end of her life, she made the comment, "I love Jesus so much, but I don't think I ever really did much for Him." I almost fell over. How could she have thought such a thing? She lived a quiet life, yes, but an incredibly faithful life. Everything she did reflected a servant's heart. She was the most steadfast example of a Christian I've ever seen. Quiet? Yes. Ineffective? Never.

Don't ever let anyone convince you that you don't have anything of value to give. Little is much in the eyes of God!

Heavenly Father, as I go about my daily tasks,
keep me centered on You.
May everything I do be from a heart of servanthood and gratitude,
and may I bless others with a whisper of Your love.

...stand fast in the faith...
—1 Corinthians 16:3

JULY 2

How often when someone asks how you're doing do you reply, "Oh, I'm hanging in there." It's a pretty common response, and I never thought much about it until a minister said from the pulpit, "Why are we 'hanging in' when we can stand on the Rock of Ages?" Good question.

Sometimes, when circumstances are tough, we might feel like we're barely holding on, but even one toe planted on the Rock gives us enough strength to endure. Either faith is worth everything or it's worth nothing—there can't be a middle ground when it comes to trusting Jesus. Stand fast. Show the world from whence cometh your help. You might be the very witness someone needs to see faith in action.

Heavenly Father, thank You for strength to stand fast.
Grow me in dependability, and let me
be an encouragement to those I encounter.

Let all your things be done with charity.
—1 Corinthians 16:14

JULY 3

Remember the song from the '70s, "...they will know we are Christian by our love..."?

It's easy to love lovable people. It's the stinkers who make it tough.

Honestly, there is nothing wrong with righteous anger. When sin runs rampant and wrongs prevail, it can stir anger in our souls. But if we're tempted to let anger give way to harsh words and rough treatment, we have to exercise caution. The Bible advises us to be angry but sin not. God knows we are human and we will experience anger. But we need to control our actions and reactions. Remembering the sinner is lost and in need of grace can help guide our reactions and prevent anger from directing us.

Heavenly Father, help me love with Your love when mine is gone. Keep me from letting anger lead me to sinful behavior.

> One thing have I desired of the Lord, that will I seek after; that I may dwell in the house of the Lord all the days of my life, to behold the beauty of the Lord...
> —Psalm 27:4

JULY 4

When I see something beautiful or majestic, I gasp (apparently I inherited this from my maternal grandmother who, according to my mother, could inhale every molecule of oxygen from a room). The Hubs and I stood high the Bavarian Alps and gazed across an endless expanse of breathtakingly beautiful mountains and valleys. I almost hyperventilated from all my gasps of wonder. And yet, the Bavarian Alps pale in comparison to the view I will one day see when I reach heaven.

Think of it: To see His face? To gaze on the scars in His hands and feet—evidence of His love for me? I doubt I will have breath enough to gasp. I'll be too busy weeping and laughing for joy at the beauty of the Lord.

---

*Heavenly Father, the beauty of Your Son's sacrifice for me
is too awesome for me to contemplate.
Thank You for the joy I have now,
and the joy I will know then.*

And thou, Solomon my son, know thou the God of thy father, and serve him with a perfect heart and with a willing mind: for the Lord searcheth all hearts, and understandeth all the imaginations of the thoughts: if thou seek him, he will be found of thee; but if thou forsake him, he will cast thee off for ever.
—1 Chronicles 28:9

JULY 5

These are words spoken to Solomon by his father, David, but they are a beautiful reminder for every believer. So often we get caught up in "going through the motions" rather than genuinely living our faith. God looks beneath the surface to our heart attitude, and He knows if we're serving Him out of habit, bitter obligation, or guilt. But when we give God our wholehearted devotion, it changes us from the inside out. Our fruit will be plentiful, our peace will flow, our joy will be complete.

---

*Heavenly Father, grow in me a heart so pure
and full of love for You that serving You
is as natural as breathing.*

Seek the Lord and his strength, seek his face continually.
—1 Chronicles 16:11

JULY 6

*E*very December since 1999, I've prayed for a Scripture to carry me through the upcoming new year. In 2004, God gave me 1 Chronicles 16:11. And what a year it was! I can't tell you how many times I wanted to wallow in despair, to roll over and give up. God knew what He was doing when He set that verse in my heart. Again and again circumstances tried to overwhelm me, but I repeated the verse and did what it said—sought His face, looked to Him and His strength—and every time my focus shifted from the problem to the problem-solver, circumstances took a backseat to His power and presence.

If you're in a desert land right now, don't give up. Instead, look up and seek His face. His strength is your enough.

---

*Heavenly Father, thank You for Your strength,
which is always sufficient to match my trial.
Remind me that nothing is too difficult for You.*

For the Lord thy God blesseth thee, as he promised thee...
—Deuteronomy 15:6a

JULY 7

I love the word "promise." Doesn't it conjure pleasant images and memories? When people keep their promises to us, we feel valued. Keeping promises builds trust. Well, guess what? God keeps His promises. He is good and faithful, and—truth!—He values *you* beyond all measure. If God says it, you can believe it. And that means you can trust Him to meet your needs and to love you forever.

---

*Heavenly Father, thank You for promising
to never leave me nor forsake me.
May I rest confidently in the truth
of Your love and concern for me.*

Behold, the Lord cometh with ten thousands of his saints, To execute judgment upon all, and to convince all that are ungodly among them of all their ungodly deeds which they have ungodly committed...
—Jude 1:14b-15a

JULY 8

There is another promise God made that can make some feel a little unsettled. One day, He will judge the world. Those who have chosen to live for self, to ignore His guidance, and to reject His Son will face God's wrath and punishment. On that day, no one will doubt God is who He said He is, but it will be too late to change their minds.

Every day the time of Christ's return draws closer. We need to pray for those we love who are still lost. We need to share the truth. The day of judgment is coming—God promised it, and He keeps His promises. We need to be ready.

---

*Heavenly Father, if there is any displeasing manner in me, please rid me of it.
May I be found flawless when You come.*

I go to prepare a place for you.
—John 14:2b

JULY 9

When Jesus left His disciples, He promised to prepare a place for them to spend eternity. The promise applies to today's believers, too. There is such comfort in knowing a mansion waits for me in Heaven. There is such hope in knowing the ones I love who've left this life are already there with Jesus, and I will see them again someday. This statement—"I go...for you"—is intensely personal. Jesus paved the way for us to reach eternity.

There's a song a lady from church sang several years ago that has resonated with me. One line says "When You were on the cross, I was on Your mind." Jesus loved us enough to die for us; He loves us enough to wait for us. Never doubt: you are loved.

---

*Heavenly Father, I long for the day
when I will reside with You forever.
Until then, hold me close and guide me.
May I direct others to You.*

And the LORD, he it is that doth go before thee; he will be with thee, he will not fail thee, neither forsake thee: fear not, neither be dismayed.
—Deuteronomy 31:8

JULY 10

Anyone who knows me knows I love the old hymns. "Standing on the Promises" by Russell K. Carter is a favorite. Read the second verse:

> Standing on the promises that cannot fail,
> When the howling storms of doubt and fear assail,
> By the living Word of God I shall prevail,
> Standing on the promises of God.

We can prevail in the midst of storms because we know God's promises are sure. He goes before us. He will not forsake us. We never have to shake our heads in dismay and fear that all is lost, because God already has our victory. We can stand sure on the promises of God!

---

*Heavenly Father, I trust Your promises are true.
Thank You for holding me safe and secure
even during life's fiercest storms.*

> *There failed not ought of any good thing which the LORD had spoken unto the house of Israel; all came to pass.*
> —Joshua 21:45

JULY 11

My grandmother believed the biblical assurance that if she raised her children in the way they should go, when they were old they wouldn't depart from it. Every day she prayed salvation for her four children. She died when my mom was only ten, but my mother accepted Jesus as Savior at the age of five. Mom's sister Lois and brother Carl were also saved before my grandmother passed away, but her oldest brother was not. But many years later he committed his way to the Lord. My grandmother's prayers were honored long after she'd gone to heaven.

All of His promises come to pass. Never doubt—the good things He speaks will occur.

---

*Heavenly Father, thank You for mothers
and grandmothers who pray.
May their pleas for salvation be honored
and Your name glorified.*

And let the peace of God rule in your hearts, to the which also ye are called in one body; and be ye thankful.
—Colossians 3:15

JULY 12

I would so much rather have peace in my heart than have worry or strife or anger or resentment or fear. I dislike contention very much—especially with those who matter to me. I would imagine I'm not the only one who feels that way! If you're at odds with a brother or sister in Christ, please take the steps to restore the relationship. If you're at odds with God, definitely take the steps to restore the relationship. We can't be at peace when our souls are in conflict with our Father or another of His children. "Let the peace of Christ rule" in your heart... What a beautiful concept.

---

*Heavenly Father, hold me close in fellowship with You.
Help me restore broken relationships
in my family or church membership.
Be honored in the way I interact with others.*

Let the word of Christ dwell in you richly in all wisdom; teaching and admonishing one another in psalms and hymns and spiritual songs, singing with grace in your hearts to the Lord.
—Colossians 3:16

JULY 13

When someone behaved in an ugly way, instead of being critical, my mom used to say, "They must be very sad on the inside, or their outsides would be happier."

When the love of Christ abides inside us, it can't help but come out. Sometimes it escapes in the form of an admonishment meant to draw a wayward believer from a path of destruction. It might not feel like love to the one receiving the correction in that moment, but if we continue to lavish care on that person they will come to see our words come from a desire to restore rather than condemn.

Keep your spirit in tune with God's by communicating with Him, praising Him, and listening to Him. When we are close to Him, we reflect Him, and His love comes through us even in the toughest moments.

---

*Heavenly Father, fill me up
so You spill from my mouth and my heart.*

Forbearing one another, and forgiving one another,
if any man have a quarrel against any: even as Christ forgave you, so also do ye.
—Colossians 3:13

JULY 14

It can be very hard to forgive someone who has hurt or offended us. To be perfectly frank, I can forgive someone who hurt me much more easily than someone who hurt one of my children. But the Lord readily forgives me. I am expected, as His chid, to follow His example.

The thing is, when we hold to resentment, we are giving the perpetrator of the hurtful deed control over us. Wouldn't we rather be in the control of the Holy Spirit? Forgiveness shifts the power from the one who hurt us to the One who comforts us. That's a much better place to rest.

Heavenly Father, if I'm holding onto anger
or resentment toward someone,
please help me follow Your example and forgive them.
Thank You for always forgiving me.

Put on therefore, as the elect of God, holy and beloved, bowels of mercies, kindness, humbleness of mind, meekness, longsuffering;
—Colossians 3:12

JULY 15

I believe it was Mark Twain who said that "clothes make the man," and to a certain extent it's true. (My fifth grade students behaved completely differently on "dress up" day as compared to "pajama day"—something about attiring oneself in formal apparel leads to more formal conduct.) As God's people, we are instructed to clothe ourselves in conduct that leaves a positive impact on those we encounter. God asks us to take on the coverings of compassion, kindness, humility, gentleness, and patience. If we have Him on our inside, then these characteristics should show on the outside. Our kind, compassionate treatment of others then leads the lost to the One who loves them dearly.

Heavenly Father, endow me with Your character, and help me treat others in the way that best reflects the example of Your Son.

Therefore being justified by faith, we have peace with God through our Lord Jesus Christ:
—Romans 5:1

JULY 16

"Peace" is a scarce commodity in the world today. Jesus came to bring peace. He told his followers, "Peace I leave with you, my peace I give unto you: not as the world giveth, give I unto you." But then, in seeming contradiction, He also said, "Suppose ye that I am come to give peace on earth? I tell you, Nay; but rather division."

Here's the thing. He provides the means for us to achieve peace *with God* through knowing we are saved and that heaven is waiting. But He acknowledged the world will never accept Him or, by default, His followers, so we can expect to be in conflict with those who oppose Him. But when we have the assurance of eternity with Him, then nothing of this world can shake us from our foundation of faith. That's the gift of "peace that passeth understanding" for all who believe.

Heavenly Father, Your Son is the Prince of Peace. Thank You for giving us peace even in this unsettled world in which we live.

And hope maketh not ashamed; because the love of God is shed abroad in our hearts by the Holy Ghost which is given unto us.
—Romans 5:5

JULY 17

Sometimes when we want something to happen we say, rather wistfully, "Oh, I hope so." But there's not a great deal of assurance behind it. "Uncertain" isn't a correct definition for the hope that God gives. Christian hope is the confident expectation in what God has promised. Its strength relies on His faithfulness. Can anything that comes from God disappoint? Not possible!

Hope is such an incredible gift. The constant, strengthening, discerning presence of the Holy Spirit is a wonderful source of hope—we are never alone as we walk in this world. Things of the world can disappoint us, but nothing that comes from God disappoints. Remember you are loved and you are never without hope.

Heavenly Father, thank You for the hope I possess and will always possess because I am Your child.

And not only so, but we glory in tribulations also: knowing that tribulation worketh patience; And patience, experience; and experience, hope:
—Romans 5:3-4

JULY 18

When was the last time you thanked God for allowing you to face a time of affliction? It isn't easy to be grateful for difficult situations, but look at what difficulties accomplish in our lives—patience (endurance!), experience (a witness to others!), and my favorite word of all: hope (the assurance of blessings yet unseen). There is a purpose in suffering. Suffering lets us lean more heavily on our Maker and lets us draw on His strength. It deepens our relationship with Him. And it leads us to another of God's wonderful gifts, *hope*. So if you're facing a trial today, turn your face skyward and thank the Lord for giving you an opportunity to grow in Him.

Heavenly Father, thank You for the blessings that grow from times of tribulation. May I be a witness to Your strength and bring glory to Your Name.

But God commendeth his love toward us, in that, while we were yet sinners, Christ died for us.
—Romans 5:8

JULY 19

One of my grandboys, who is more intellectual than athletic, decided he needed to be more active. So he joined the school cross country team. New to running, he had a hard time keeping up with kids who'd already participated in the sport for a year or more. His teammates weren't as encouraging as they should have been, and discouragement got the better of him. He dropped out.

Those cross country kids wanted someone already proficient at running on their team. Thank goodness God doesn't operate that way. He doesn't expect us to already be "proficient" at holiness. While we were mired in sin, He sent His Son to the cross for us. We never have to worry about not being "good enough" for God; He takes us where we are and welcomes us with open arms.

---

*Heavenly Father, thank You for loving me
even in my weakness and brokenness
and claiming me as Your own.*

> By whom also we have access by faith into this grace wherein we stand, and rejoice in hope of the glory of God.
> —Romans 5:2

JULY 20

Sometimes people think, "I've fallen too far away from God to go Home again." Not so! No matter how badly we've failed, how far we've drifted into sin, God's grace is still available. We can be given a clean slate to start again. *I once was lost, but now I'm found.* We don't have to hide in shame and self-recrimination—God's grace covers all.

Heavenly Father, thank You for Your boundless grace which erases all of my sin.

Declaring the end from the beginning, and from ancient times the things that are not yet done, saying, My counsel shall stand, and I will do all my pleasure:
—Isaiah 46:10

JULY 21

Consider this: from the beginning of time, God had a plan for your life that would bring you complete fulfillment and joy even in the midst of difficulty. That plan was to send Jesus into this world to save you from your sins, redeem you, and make you holy. Oh, you can ignore Him and choose your own pathway. But that doesn't change the fact that God sent Jesus for you. He did His part, all the way to the cross. An old hymn includes these words as if from Jesus Himself: "I gave My life to ransom thee, Surrender your all today." We find His plan for us when we surrender to Him.

Are you holding something back? If so, lay it at His feet. Discover the joy of committing fully to the One who has loved you since before time began.

---

*Heavenly Father, Your love for me is boundless.
Take me—heart, mind, and soul—and guide me in Your pathway.
I trust my all to You.*

> **Look unto me, and be ye saved, all the ends of the earth: for I am God, and there is none else.**
> —Isaiah 45:22

JULY 22

"Turn Your Eyes Upon Jesus" by Helen Lemmel is one of my favorite hymns. A line from verse two really speaks to me: "O'er us sin no more hath dominion, for more than conqu'rors we are!"

He is GOD. There is none else above Him. We are His children—His redeemed! As His adopted sons and daughters, we can call Him Abba, and because of His Son we have conquered sin. No need to fear damnation. No need to hide our heads in shame. No need to scramble around trying to curry favors. We're saved for all eternity by Yahweh, the Covenant God. In moments when uncertainty or doubt try to plague you, turn your eyes upon Jesus. Look full in His wonderful face. Remember that you are redeemed by the Blood of the Lamb, and the things of earth will shatter in the light of His glory and grace.

Heavenly Father, You have given me victory over sin's curse. It has no hold on me. Thank You, Lord, for saving me!

...there is no God else beside me; a just God and a Saviour; there is none beside me.
—Isaiah 45:21c

JULY 23

The "all paths lead to God" theory ruffles my feathers and—even more than that—saddens me. There is only one true God, and He sent Jesus into this world to be our Mediator. If you don't go through Jesus to get to God, you won't get there. Period. People can do their best to water things down and make the message so bland no one will question it, but here's the truth: only one pathway leads to the one true God...and He is Savior, Master, Redeemer, Lord. His name is *Jesus*.

Heavenly Father, You are the one true God.
I will love You and serve You—only You—for all of my days.

For thus saith the Lord that created the heavens; God himself that formed the earth and made it; he hath established it, he created it not in vain, he formed it to be inhabited: I am the Lord; and there is none else.
—Isaiah 45:18

JULY 24

God is the Creator. There was no "big bang," no "it just happened," no "cells divided and something else was formed." He meticulously crafted this world so all parts worked together with an intricacy it has taken scientists centuries to fully comprehend. He did it not for His enjoyment, but for ours. He designed the perfect habitat for us, providing everything we need for our bodies, spirits, and souls. Nothing we see, hear, smell, touch, or taste is by chance—it is all a gift from Yahweh. If someone tries to tell you otherwise, read Isaiah 45:18 to them. The truth could set them free.

Heavenly Father, guard me from accepting man's logic over the truth of Your Word.
Thank You for Your wonderful creation.
May I be a good steward of what we've been given.

Pray ye therefore the Lord of the harvest, that he will send forth labourers into his harvest.
—Matthew 9:38

JULY 25

Have you ever stopped to consider that you are a missionary? "Missionary" is defined, in part, as a person strongly in favor of a set of principles, who attempts to persuade others. Consequently, any believer who shares the Gospel is a missionary.

We need to pray for field missionaries—those who travel far from home to spread the good news of Jesus—and we need to pray for ourselves to have the courage to share when the Holy Spirit provides an opportunity. All believers are His workers, so let's march across this harvest field!

Heavenly Father, thank You for the good news available to all people everywhere. Give me the opportunity and the courage to share Your message of salvation.

According to my earnest expectation and my hope, that in nothing I shall be ashamed, but that with all boldness, as always, so now also Christ shall be magnified in my body, whether it be by life, or by death.
—Philippians 1:20

JULY 26

I'm a very mild-mannered person, non-combatant, one who prefers to avoid conflict. But "dis" someone I love and watch my claws come out. You don't hurt one of mine and come away unscathed. The above might fit you, too. Now think about this… I love Jesus. He hung on a cross in excruciating pain to take the penalty for my sins. He is *my* Savior. He is *my* Lord. When someone speaks ill of Him, do my claws come out? Do I speak in defense of Him?

If we defend Jesus, we will likely offend someone. But we still need to speak up and pronounce the truth: Jesus is the Way, the Truth, and the Life. Let's not water that message down to make it palatable. The Truth sets people free!

Heavenly Father, give me the courage to speak the truth about Jesus in love so all will know the joy and assurance found in a relationship with Your Son.

And, behold, a woman, which was diseased with an issue of blood twelve years, came behind him, and touched the hem of his garment: For she said within herself, If I may but touch his garment, I shall be whole. But Jesus turned... and when he saw her, he said, Daughter, be of good comfort; thy faith hath made thee whole. And the woman was made whole from that hour.
—Matthew 9:20-21

JULY 27

The reference to this woman is so brief—it would be easy to overlook in the broad scheme of Jesus' ministry. It's also one of my favorite passages in the Bible. After suffering physically (from the condition) and emotionally (from the likely ostracism) for more than a decade of her life, she still gathered up enough courage to move through the crowds, to reach out, and to touch the hem of Jesus' robe.

He recognized the faith it had taken, and *in that moment* she was healed. I don't even know her name, but she inspires me to be courageous, to reach out, and to trust. "...thy faith hath made thee whole." Beautiful, beautiful words...

Heavenly Father, give me the faith to reach out with the expectation of being made whole through Your touch.

That ye may approve things that are excellent; that ye may be sincere and without offence till the day of Christ. Being filled with the fruits of righteousness, which are by Jesus Christ, unto the glory and praise of God.
—Philippians 1:10-11

JULY 28

We live in a world that doesn't honor God. (Speak the name Jesus and see how quickly some rise to offense.) Consequently, we are constantly bombarded by influences that are not what God intended for us. We need to weed those things from our lives. How do we know whether something is God-approved or not? Search His word. Ask the Holy Spirit to give you discernment. Ask yourself, "Does this bring glory to my Savior?" One day we will stand before God at the end of our time on earth. May our greatest reward be hearing those wonderful words: "Well done, thou good and faithful servant."

Heavenly Father, in this world of temptations, guard my mind and my heart to honor You in my thoughts and actions.

And Jesus went about all the cities and villages, teaching in their synagogues, and preaching the gospel of the kingdom, and healing every sickness and every disease among the people.
—Matthew 9:35

JULY 29

There are many things to admire about Jesus and I won't even try to list them all. But one of the most important, in my opinion, was His lack of prejudice. Jews, Gentiles, Publicans, religious leaders, those who already followed God and those who lived wretched lives... no matter the person, He offered the same opportunity for salvation.

It's so easy for us to put people into categories and then sit in the box that seems to fit us the best. We need the fellowship and accountability of Christian brothers and sisters, but if we "stick with our kind," how will we make a difference? Yes, it can be awkward and uncomfortable, but start with a smile. A simple hello. Who knows how God might use your willingness to reach out?

Heavenly Father, help me step beyond my comfort zones and extend a hand of welcome to those who seem different to me. Let me love with Your love.

But when he saw the multitudes, he was moved with compassion on them, because they fainted, and were scattered abroad, as sheep having no shepherd.
—Matthew 9:36

JULY 30

Compassion goes beyond feeling sorry for others to actually feeling the pain they are going through. Jesus was very compassionate. He looked upon the great groups of people and realized they were lost--destined to eternal separation from God the Father—and it broke His heart.

Several years ago I began praying "break my heart for what breaks Yours." When I saw people being disrespectful or impatient or rude, sometimes I wanted to tell them to straighten up. Now I think *They lack guidance and need attention;* or *They're overwhelmed;* or *They must've had an awful day.* Most of all, I'm reminded they are lost and need a Shepherd. That simple prayer has softened my heart, and I'm so grateful, even though sometimes it can sure make my chest ache.

---

*Heavenly Father,
let me truly see the needs and weaknesses of those around me.*

*If any of you lack wisdom,
let him ask of God,
that giveth to all men liberally,
and upbraideth not;
and it shall be given him.*
—James 1:5

JULY 31

I've considered joining Over-thinkers Anonymous—you know: "My name is Kim, and I live in the state of uncertainty." Sometimes I have a hard time making decisions. I bounce things around in my mind, weighing every possible scenario, and even then, I can still be stuck in limbo.

Knowledge, judgment, discernment... We all need it. Sometimes people get impatient when we ask questions, but—thank goodness!—God isn't people. When we need wisdom to make God-honoring decisions, He is always willing to give us the answers we need. It's His desire for us to walk on Godly pathways of good, so He never sends us in the wrong direction.

On second thought, I don't need Over-thinkers Anonymous. I just need time in prayer and an open heart to heed His direction.

Heavenly Father, thank You for Your patient guidance.

> Being confident of this very thing, that he which hath begun a good work in you will perform it until the day of Jesus Christ:
> —Philippians 1:6

AUGUST 1

God's plans are always for our good and for His glory. Because we are trapped in human skin, we sometimes stumble along pathways that aren't what He would choose for us. But He doesn't give up on us. The minute we turn our eyes heavenward and say, "Father, guide me," He will.

This scripture also reminds us to not be impatient. I wanted to be a published author from the time I was five years old; my first book released forty years after I told my kindergarten teacher that people would check out my book from a library. During those ensuing years I often longed to see my dream culminated, but in retrospect, His timing was perfect. It always is.

So my advice? Don't give up on yourself, and don't run ahead of Him. He truly will bring to you to the ideal place of completion.

Heavenly Father, give me the confidence
to follow You and trust Your timing.
Thank You for loving me enough to guide and direct me.

O LORD our God, other lords beside thee have had dominion over us: but by thee only will we make mention of thy name.
—Isaiah 26:13

AUGUST 2

Obeying our governing laws is important. Negative consequences await those who choose to ignore laws. But greater consequences—those with eternal impact—affect those who place anything above God. God is our Creator. He made us, and He made wonderful plans for our lives. When we shove Him to the side in lieu of things of the world's making, we lose the blessings He wants to bestow on us. We lose our close fellowship with the One who made us in His image. Obey the laws of land…as long as they aren't in opposition to the God's Word.

Heavenly Father, please let there be no god in my life taking precedence over the One True God in my heart!

Then saith he unto his disciples, The harvest truly is plenteous, but the labourers are few;
—Matthew 9:37

AUGUST 3

Since I started praying "break my heart for what breaks Yours," my heart has begun literally aching when I think about the lost souls wandering my neighborhood, my state, my country, this world. These people are hopeless and destined for eternal damnation.

We don't know how much time any of us have left in this world. Death most often comes unannounced. The Lord could return. Since we are on borrowed time, we must take advantage of the minutes we have to share the message of salvation with those who need it. In this season of "tolerance," telling someone he is lost isn't considered politically correct, but I don't think we should be nearly as concerned about being politically correct as we are with sharing the truth. This world *needs* Jesus.

Heavenly Father, thank You for the assurance of my salvation. Embolden me to share You with those who are lost. Let my life point others to You.

> ...inasmuch as both in my bonds, and in the defence and confirmation of the gospel, ye all are partakers of my grace.
> —Philippians 1:6

AUGUST 4

Being a Christian is not taking the easy road. Christianity is a narrow path, and few take it (see Matthew 7:13-14). Because it's so much easier to follow the world's examples than the ones provided by Jesus, it is so important for us not to travel the pathway on our own. Yes, we have the Holy Spirit who helps us, but we also benefit from the support of fellow brothers and sisters in Christ. They encourage us, counsel us, and hold us accountable.

Do you have prayer partners in your life? If not, ask God to lead you to some. We all need someone who "has our back."

Heavenly Father, thank You for the power of prayer.
Let me be a support to my Christian family and friends,
and open others' hearts to pray for me.
May You find us faithful.

*Yea, in the way of thy judgments,
O LORD, have we waited for thee;
the desire of our soul is to thy name,
and to the remembrance of thee.*
—Isaiah 26:8

AUGUST 5

Waiting isn't easy for most people. Remember Veruca from *Willie Wonka and the Chocolate Factory*? She always hollered, "I want it *now!*" Most often, when we want something, we want it *now*. But there's a reason patience is considered a virtue.

When we learn to do what God has instructed and wait for His timing, we learn a deeper trust. When we seek Him and His ways above everything else, our hearts experience a deeper joy. Today's scripture makes a perfect prayer—if you speak it and mean it, what you're saying is you trust God to work His will in and through you. Choosing to trust that He knows best will bless you beyond all expectation.

---

*Heavenly Father, as my soul pines for things yet unclaimed,
let me trust You to do what is best for me
and for those I love.*

> Trust ye in the LORD for ever:
> for in the LORD JEHOVAH
> is everlasting strength:
> —Isaiah 26:4

AUGUST 6

Nothing in and of this world is forever. (Not even diamonds, no matter what the song tries to tell you.) Everything—relationships, jobs, houses, emotions, belongings...—is temporal *except* our relationship with God through His Son Jesus Christ. Putting our hope or confidence or trust in anything but Him will lead to disappointment, because eventually whatever that "thing" is, it won't be there for you someday. But *He* is our Rock eternal!

Stand firm on Him and His teachings, and your way will be secure.

---

*Heavenly Father, let my trust be in You and You alone,
for You alone are worthy of my confidence.*

For he hath made him to be sin for us, who knew no sin; that we might be made the righteousness of God in him.
—2 Corinthians 5:21

AUGUST 7

Do you ever worry you aren't "good enough" for God? Well, stop that! I don't mean stop trying to emulate Him. Our call as believers is to be "little Christs." But stop *worrying* about falling short. We don't have to be good enough. In fact, we're wise to openly acknowledge that we aren't good enough. Because if we were "good enough," we'd have no need for a Savior.

Christ came. He lived, He died *for us*, He rose again, and now He intercedes for us. When we accept His gift of salvation, we become righteous. Holy. Clean. The full truth is, we can never be "good enough," but—thank You, Jesus!—His goodness is enough to cover us.

Heavenly Father, thank You for Your Son whose goodness is enough to cover my imperfections.

> ...be ye reconciled to God.
> —2 Corinthians 5:20c

AUGUST 8

"Let he who is without sin cast the first stone!" If someone has said that to you, they likely delivered it in a tone of anger or defensiveness.

It's scary to tell someone they're walking a path to destruction. Partly because we're all sinners and the other person has every right and reason to point a finger of blame right back at us. But telling someone "You're lost and you need a Savior" isn't casting a stone; it's casting a life preserver. Thanks to Christ, I am saved by grace. My sins have been washed clean. I have been reconciled to God. And, oh, how I long for those who are still entangled in sin to receive that cleansing.

Christ died to save. On His behalf, share the message. God desires reconciliation with every lost soul.

---

*Heavenly Father, thank You for saving me
from sin's destruction.
Give me the courage to share Your saving grace
with those who are still caught in sin's snares.*

> *For we know that if our earthly house of this tabernacle were dissolved, we have a building of God, an house not made with hands, eternal in the heavens.*
> —2 Corinthians 5:1

AUGUST 9

Paul, who wrote these words, was a tentmaker, thus familiar with temporary housing. But here he isn't referencing a structure but our mortal body. If we live to old age, our bodies will break down. If Jesus doesn't come first, we will face physical death. And Paul makes death sound no more devastating than a tent collapse.

Having our "house" dissolve isn't devastating when we know our soul belongs to Him. Our shell might dissolve, but our soul will last eternally. I had the privilege of being with my mom when her soul fled her broken body, and the assurance that she was graduating directly to heaven gave me joy in the midst of my sorrow.

You have an eternal place in heaven that will never tarnish nor deteriorate. I hope that reminder brings you comfort as you reside in your "tent" today.

Heavenly Father, Your assurances are beautiful.
Thank You for readying my soul for eternity with You.

Thou wilt keep him in perfect peace, whose mind is stayed on thee: because he trusteth in thee.
—Isaiah 26:3

AUGUST 10

I love God's promises, because I know I can count on them. I read Isaiah 26:3 as a promise, too. If we keep our focus on God—His strength, His presence, His purpose—then we're less likely to be pulled into an attitude of despair. One of His greatest gifts to us is peace in the midst of a storm.

If it's "storming" in your life right now, turn your eyes heavenward. Remember His promises to never leave you nor forsake you and to give you strength as your days require it. Peace will descend.

---

*Heavenly Father, in the presence of Jehovah
I find my peace and rest.*

> Wherefore we labour, that, whether present or absent, we may be accepted of him.
> —2 Corinthians 5:9

AUGUST 11

"...Be accepted of Him." To me, those are the most important words in this scripture. We get pulled in so many directions by peers and family members and employers and the government and even strangers on the street. We make choices every day whether to stay quiet and avoid conflict or speak up and face condemnation. If we make it our aim to please Him, we will be called names and rejected and be considered a fool. But if we endure, if we choose *Him* and *His ways* over all else, we can move forward with a clear conscience.

The world is temporary; our relationship with Him is eternal. Which bears the greatest importance?

Heavenly Father, help me choose wisely both what I say and what I do, making my best effort to please You.

Knowing therefore the terror of the Lord, we persuade men; but we are made manifest unto God; and I trust also are made manifest in your consciences.
—2 Corinthians 5:11

AUGUST 12

If we know the truth (and we can know the truth by reading the Bible, God's inerrant words), we have an obligation to share it. People are lost! If we knew someone was about to fall over a cliff to his death, would we think, "Oh, grabbing him would offend him" and let him fall? Of course not—that would be heartless. But when we refuse to share the truth, we're essentially allowing the lost to face eternal separation from God. We must be open before God. We must be open before men. Not to condemn or to judge, but to convict and to save. We persuade by speaking the truth in *love*.

---

*Heavenly Father, You are a God of love
and a God of righteous judgment.
Let me share Your love truthfully
so those I know and care about will be free
from sin's damnation.*

Wherein I suffer trouble, as an evil doer, even unto bonds; but the word of God is not bound.
—2 Timothy 2:9

AUGUST 13

There are many forces right now trying to squelch the gospel. We can't talk about Christianity in schools or in businesses, can't pray before ballgames or graduations without someone complaining. It frustrates me when these things happen, but then when I stop and really think about it, amusement rises. Do these people really believe they can stop God's message from reaching people's hearts? Paul's message continued to go out even while he was locked up in a prison cell for talking about Jesus!

God isn't affected by government laws or people's prejudices. They might bind the messenger, but they can't bind the Message. God's Word *will* prevail!

Heavenly Father, in those moments when it seems hope is gone, remind me that Your Word is mightier than man's efforts to squelch it.

Hold fast the form of sound words, which thou hast heard of me, in faith and love which is in Christ Jesus.
—2 Timothy 1:13

AUGUST 14

When hardships—unexpected events, losses we don't understand, tragedy—affect us, we have two choices: turn our backs on faith or stand firm on what we've learned about faith. When we choose the former rather than the latter, we leave ourselves floundering in our own strength.

I don't know about you, but I know for sure I'm a weakling. When I sing with my grandchildren, "...they are weak, but He is strong," I totally nod, because I know the truth of it too well. Jesus loves us, (which I also know!), but that doesn't mean we won't face difficult situations. However, it does mean He will be our strength, and He will be there to carry us through.

Hold on to your faith! Jesus' strength and love will sustain you.

---

*Heavenly Father, thank You
for letting me tap into Your strength when I am weak.
Your strength is enough.*

Be not thou therefore ashamed of the testimony of our Lord, nor of me his prisoner: but be thou partaker of the afflictions of the gospel according to the power of God;
—2 Timothy 1:8

AUGUST 15

Most of us wouldn't proclaim with pride that we spent time in prison. It's not likely something we'd put in the annual Christmas-card letter, either. But in Paul's case, there was no reason for shame. He landed in jail because he refused to be silenced about Jesus. There are Christians in foreign lands who are, right now, stuck in a jail cell for the same reason that Paul faced imprisonment. I hope their family members aren't ashamed of them for taking such a stand.

If Christianity was outlawed in America, would you have the courage to continue to share your faith even if you knew it could land you in jail? Being imprisoned for telling someone how Jesus saves is so much better than being caught in sin's grip. We will likely, at some point in our Christian walk, suffer recrimination for our faith in Jesus. Paul was willing to suffer for the sake of the Gospel. I pray we are willing, too.

---

*Heavenly Father, You give so much.
May I stand for You even against opposition and mistreatment.
Give me the strength to proclaim Your Son's Name.*

> Blessed is the man that walketh not in the counsel of the ungodly, nor standeth in the way of sinners, nor sitteth in the seat of the scornful. But his delight is in the law of the Lord; and in his law doth he meditate day and night. And he shall be like a tree planted by the rivers of water, that bringeth forth his fruit in his season; his leaf also shall not wither; and whatsoever he doeth shall prosper.
> —Psalm 1:1-3

AUGUST 16

Who doesn't want to prosper? When we think of prosperity, we often consider finances. Sure, it's nice to have enough money and then some, but there's a prosperity much more important than a big bank account: the prosperity of faith.

We prosper spiritually when we dig our roots down deep into the water of God's Word and saturate ourselves with the knowledge found in His book. In prayer, ask God for discernment. Delight in serving Him by living in a way that pleases Him. Your soul will not wither, and you will be spiritually prosperous. This is prosperity that lasts into eternity—the very best prosperity!

Heavenly Father, thank You for the truth of Your Word.
May I hide Your Word in my heart
so I might live in a way that glorifies You
and brings me spiritual prosperity.

> *For ye shall go out with joy,
> and be led forth with peace:
> the mountains and the hills
> shall break forth before you
> into singing, and all the trees
> of the field shall
> clap their hands.*
> —Isaiah 55:12

AUGUST 17

I can't read this scripture without wanting to sing it. Isaiah was prophesying about the children of Israel's entry into the promised land. When they crossed that threshold and claimed the land that had been guaranteed to them by Yahweh, they would enter it with joy.

We have a promised land waiting, too: Heaven. And when we reach our promised land, we will enter with joy, I have no doubt! No sorrow, no tears, no crying there! I long for that day. But until we reach heaven's gate, we can also live with joy. Let the unsaved see the difference it makes to anchor one's hope in the Lord. Share His love so others might come to believe. Burst into song and praise Him for the joy and peace He gives. This hungry, hurting world needs our Savior.

---

*Heavenly Father, thank You for preparing heaven
as an eternal home for all who call You Father.
May heaven's joy reside in my heart now
and spill over so all will desire a relationship with You.*

I have set the LORD always before me: because he is at my right hand, I shall not be moved.
—Psalm 16:8

AUGUST 18

When I was a kid, our family moved a lot. I was bashful, and entering yet another classroom full of strangers was hard. Sixth grade was the toughest, because I'd been in the previous school for three years, and I'd come to feel comfortable there. I wanted to say, "I shall not be moved!" On the first day of sixth grade, my mom prayed for me to be courageous. She reminded me that I wasn't walking into the classroom alone—God went with me, and He wouldn't leave me on my own.

Countless times in my adult life I've remembered Mom's assurance, and I've envisioned Him "going before me" as I interviewed for jobs, began new places of employment, stepped behind a podium, or even entered a jury box. There's security in knowing He is with us wherever we go. We needn't move in fear when He is by our side.

Heavenly Father, thank You for Your presence at all times. Help me depend upon Your courage in new situations and use each experience to build my trust in You.

The fruit of the righteous is a tree of life; and he that winneth souls is wise.
—Proverbs 11:30a

AUGUST 19

My dad is an amazing gardener. If you visit his house, you'll discover there are flowers even flourishing in the cracks of his driveway! If he plants a seed, it sprouts and grows. Then with the rain and sun to feed it, it bears fruit in season.

A life planted in God's Word sprouts and grows. With mercy rains and the Son's guidance, we grow, too, into righteous ones who point others to God's love. Do you feel stagnant? Perhaps you need a fresh dousing of time in the Bible, which brings us life.

---

*Heavenly Father, give me a thirst for You and Your Word.
May my roots dig deeply into Your soil
and may I bear fruit that benefits Your kingdom.*

Then shall the trees of the wood sing out at the presence of the Lord, because he cometh to judge the earth.
—1 Chronicles 16:33

AUGUST 20

My favorite tree is the willow. Its graceful, waving branches invite me to draw near and sit beneath its cooling shelter. I love how trees seem to reach for the heavens, as if striving to touch the face of God. Trees have a music, too—a whispering melody stirred by the wind. Have you ever listened to the lullaby of a tree's stirring branches? The leaves seem to gently clap together in a joyous sound, nature's way of praising God.

If the forests sing their praise, shouldn't we do likewise? For what will you praise God today?

---

*Heavenly Father, let my very life
be a song of praise lifted to You,
my Redeemer and King.*

That ye put off...the old man, which is corrupt according to the deceitful lusts; And be renewed in the spirit of your mind; And that ye put on the new man, which after God is created in righteousness and true holiness.
—Ephesians 4:22-24

AUGUST 21

My oldest daughter loves the ocean. When she and her family go on vacation, they always gravitate toward bodies of water. I'm not a beach nut (sorry...I like my air conditioning, thank you), but I do love watching waves roll in and sweep out again. Each wave that hits the beach is a totally new wave. It's fun to write something in the sand and then watch the ebb and flow erase it.

Redemption works the same way as an ocean wave. It washes away the "old man" and leaves behind a clean slate. When we confess our sin to the Father, we're given a fresh start. Change begins with a repentant heart, followed by a new attitude in our minds, and a determination to be holy (set apart) as He is holy. We don't have to remain trapped in sinful desires that do not benefit our souls. Thank the Lord for His redemption!

Heavenly Father, You are a God of new beginnings. Thank You for Your redemption, which lets me start anew each morning.

And be ye kind one to another, tenderhearted, forgiving one another, even as God for Christ's sake hath forgiven you.
—Ephesians 4:32

AUGUST 22

Putting words to music makes things easier to remember, and when I was younger, I learned this verse to a little tune. Consequently, even though I find memorization more challenging as I get older, this scripture has stuck with me. When I'm tempted to snap at someone or to hold a grudge, the Holy Spirit whispers these words to my heart: be tenderhearted; be forgiving.

God's compassion is endless. He forgave me of my grievous sins. If I truly love Him, can I do any less for others?

Heavenly Father, thank You for the reminder to be kind. Build in me a heart of compassion that reflects Your nature.

Be ye angry, and sin not: let not the sun go down upon your wrath: Neither give place to the devil.
—Ephesians 4:26-27

AUGUST 23

God gave us emotions. They're part of our make up. Anger is one of our emotions, and there will be times when we get mad. Feelings are feelings, and we can't always control how we feel. However, we can control—with the Lord's help—what we do with our feelings. If we allow an emotion to take control of us, then we've given something other than the Holy Spirit the reins of our lives.

The "let not the sun go down upon your wrath" is sound advice, too. How can we sleep well when we're tangled up in resentment and frustration? I'd rather end my day relaxed and content. Contentment is possible when we choose to forgive someone who has wronged us or confess if we've wronged someone else. Lying down with a clear conscience, free of bitterness, is a good way rest peacefully.

Heavenly Father, thank You for Jesus' example of prayer: forgive my debts, as I forgive my debtors. May my conscience be clear before You.

> *Let no corrupt communication proceed out of your mouth, but that which is good to the use of edifying, that it may minister grace unto the hearers.*
> —Ephesians 4:29

AUGUST 24

The tongue is such a small part of our body, but it can sure wreak havoc. I think most of us have said things we wish we could take back. And I've heard a few things I wish I could erase from my memory!

Corrupt communication covers a lot of bases: untruthful statements, taking the Lord's Name in vain, gossip, coarse speech, criticism, slander... When I taught fifth grade, I had a rule for the classroom: Before speaking, ponder if the words are kind, true, and necessary; if not, then keep the comment to yourself. Easier said than done...

The tongue can be pretty hard to control, but it isn't impossible. Like any other desired behavior, it takes discipline to make it a habit. But our goal as Christians should be to edify with our words, to be a minister of grace.

Heavenly Father, please season my words with Your grace.

For if we sin wilfully after that we have received the knowledge of the truth, there remaineth no more sacrifice for sins,
—Hebrews 10:26

AUGUST 25

Many years ago I overheard a mother in a church nursery say, when speaking of her three-year-old daughter, "She's at the age of getting a lot of time-outs because she knows better and misbehaves anyway."

When we know right from wrong, the expectation for appropriate behavior increases. We can't expect a non-Christian to be Christlike—they aren't indwelled with the Holy Spirit. But those who have openly repented of their sinful ways and accepted Christ's gift of salvation are held to accountability. If we know we're walking a pathway that doesn't honor God and we willingly choose to travel it anyway, we're treading a dangerous ground. We must be cautious where we place our feet. If we're uncertain, we can rely on the Spirit's guidance.

If we know better, then God expects us to do better. When we please our Father, we protect our soul.

---

*Heavenly Father, please guide and direct me.
May the path I follow always be pleasing in Your sight.*

Let us hold fast the profession of our faith without wavering; (for he is faithful that promised;)
—Hebrews 10:23

AUGUST 26

Growing up in the Mennonite church, I sang a lot of hymns. Oh, the doctrine in those stanzas! Some still resonate in my soul:

My hope is built on nothing less
Than Jesus' blood and righteousness!
I dare not trust the sweetest frame
But wholly lean on Jesus' Name.
(From "My Hope is Built on Nothing Less" by Edward Mote)

My hope isn't built on a bank account or a husband or a publisher. My hope is built on the One who was, who is, and who is yet to come. Everything else in my life will, whether intentionally or not, let me down at some point. But not my Savior. I can trust Him, because He is ever faithful. Do you wholly lean on Jesus's Name?

Heavenly Father, thank You for the assurance of salvation.
Thank You for the indwelling of Your Spirit.
I trust You to guard my soul today, tomorrow, and forever.

Let us draw near with a true heart in full assurance of faith…
—Hebrews 10:22a

AUGUST 27

My mom used to teasingly say, "There's nothing certain except death and taxes." She was right—rest assured, tax season rolls around and eventually our physical bodies wear out. But there's another assurance, one I welcome more than tax season: my Father-God is with me.

I love how available God is. He is never-changing. Whenever a lost soul reaches out, He is there to take hold and draw him near. The tiniest faith, even the size of a mustard seed, is enough when it's offered in sincerity. If you feel lost and alone, reach out. God is waiting.

---

*Heavenly Father, thank You for always being near.
You're only a prayer away!
I trust You completely to guide me through this day.*

Blessed is a man who perseveres under trial; for once he has been approved, he will receive the crown of life which the Lord has promised to those who love Him.
—James 1:2

AUGUST 28

Have you ever been driving with someone who bumped a curb with one of the car's tires and then muttered, "Curb check—it's there"? It's kind of joke with The Hubs and me.

We don't need to make curb checks, but occasionally we should make a self-check. If someone unexpectedly "bumped into" us in a store or at work or in our home, would they see that the Spirit is intact? Do I reflect Him in my words, my actions, and my attitudes? Do I live as I claim to believe? When we truly put Jesus first, those "curb checks" will reveal Him.

Heavenly Father, thank You for Your testing,
which give me a chance to grow in Your grace.
May my response to trials point to Your strength and truth.

For we walk by faith, not by sight:
—2 Corinthians 5:7a

AUGUST 29

In early 2005, when the Lord instructed me to close my classroom door, I balked because He didn't tell me where I would go. The Hubs and I had financial concerns and uncertainties galore. It took faith to turn in my resignation, but eventually God revealed His intention, and I've been so blessed.

We like to see around every bend and know what's coming next, but if we could, would we need faith? If we saw it all, how many times would fear keep us from forging forward…and consequently how many blessings would we miss? Faith takes the leap even when we can't see where we'll land. But when we land in His will, we're always on solid ground.

Heavenly Father, please give me the courage to go where You lead, even when the way seems dim. If I can't see the whole, I'll trust You to reveal it in Your perfect way and time.

> *And I will come near to you to judgment; and I will be a swift witness against the sorcerers, and against the adulterers, and against false swearers, and against those that oppress the hireling in his wages, the widow, and the fatherless, and that turn aside the stranger from his right, and fear not me, saith the Lord of hosts.*
> —Malachi 3:5

AUGUST 30

There are a whole lot of people walking around in this world with a smug grin, an absent conscience, and an all-about-me attitude. But the day will come when that grin will change to an expression of fear-filled awe, their remembrances of ill deeds will scorch like fire, and recognition that they've wasted their lives will be all too clear. And that day will be too late for them to change.

If the above paragraph depresses you, don't let it. Because, first of all, there is always hope! And tomorrow we will look at the flip side of this coin.

---

*Heavenly Father, if there is any wayward behavior
or arrogance in me, strip me of it.
Let my words, attitude, and actions reflect You.*

Then they that feared the Lord spake often one to another: and the Lord hearkened, and heard it, and a book of remembrance was written before him for them that feared the Lord, and that thought upon his name. And they shall be mine, saith the Lord of hosts, in that day when I make up my jewels; and I will spare them, as a man spareth his own son that serveth him.
—Malachi 3:16-17

AUGUST 31

The vilest offender who chooses to believe will receive a pardon. No matter how many years spent in wanton sin, how deeply one has dallied in shameful ways, a simple touch by God wipes the soul clean.

One of God's most amazing attributes, in my opinion, is His ability to forgive. When we repent and turn from our wicked ways, He restores us *in that instant* to right fellowship with Him again. But then He has an expectation: Walk better this time. When a parent disciplines a child, he expects the child to make a change in his behavior. God, as a loving Father, also wants to see us change our behavior.

He is coming to judge the world. My name will be found in His Book of Life. Is yours there, too?

*Heavenly Father, You are my Redeemer,
Sustainer, Guide, and Teacher.
Teach me Your ways and help me walk
in Your truth.*

The thief cometh not, but for to steal, and to kill, and to destroy: I am come that they might have life, and that they might have it more abundantly.
—John 10:10

SEPTEMBER 1

Some people refuse to submit to God because they don't want somebody dictating their lives. Hmm... Good luck with that. *wink* You see, we either serve our Creator, or we serve self. Serving self means being a slave to sin. When we're enslaved by sin, we're never satisfied, so life becomes a constant striving for something more or better. The worst part? When we serve self, we're accepting the enemy's lie that we don't need a Savior.

Jesus came that we might have abundant life—life to the full. One ruler seeks to destroy; the other comes to give life. Seems like a pretty simple choice, doesn't it?

---

*Heavenly Father, thank You for sending Jesus
and making it possible for me to know You personally.
Thank You for giving me abundant life—
both now and eternally.*

For we know that if our earthly house of this tabernacle were dissolved, we have a building of God, an house not made with hands, eternal in the heavens.
—2 Corinthians 5:1

SEPTEMBER 2

To me, this verse encapsulates the hope of Christianity. As the old song goes, "This world is not my home, I'm just a-passin' through; my treasures are laid up somewhere beyond the blue!" The here and now, even at its best, pales in light of eternity. Christian, this isn't all we get. We tend to consider what's waiting in heaven when heartaches and and trials and worries plague us. We remind ourselves the troubles are temporary. But the truth applies when we're dancing on the mountaintops, too.

The most wondrous day on earth can't compare with a single minute in eternity. The best is yet to come!

Heavenly Father, thank You for the promise of heaven with You, where joy will be my constant companion.

Understand therefore, that the Lord thy God giveth thee not this good land to possess it for thy righteousness; for thou art a stiffnecked people.
—Deuteronomy 9:6

SEPTEMBER 3

Moses spoke these words to the Israelites. Stiffnecked people, he called them, and he was right! They stubbornly refused to remain in a state of contentment.

Have you ever felt as though you gave and gave to someone and they just didn't appreciate it? Frustrating, isn't it? I imagine that's how God felt toward the children of Israel. The abundant blessings He rained on them, and they couldn't see the good He'd done. Sometimes we need to stop our busy running around and purposely *look* at what God is doing in our lives. We need to count our blessings and give Him praise. (And it might be good to thank the giving people in our lives, too. It's always nice to feel appreciated, right?)

Heavenly Father, thank You for all You do for me.
May I not be so stiffnecked I can't see Your goodness.
Let me develop a heart of gratitude toward You.

> *For ye have not received the spirit of bondage again to fear; but ye have received the Spirit of adoption, whereby we cry, Abba, Father.*
> —Romans 8:15

SEPTEMBER 4

Have you ever seen a child run to daddy when he is hurt or frightened? A good daddy scoops up his child, comforts him, and assures him he'll be all right because Daddy is there.

If you have accepted Christ, you are God's child. You can run to your Abba Father, knowing He will give you peace, comfort, strength, and wisdom. He enables you to walk this world in a way that glorifies Him and leaves you free of regrets. You never have to be afraid to run to God because His love is bigger than any wrongdoing and His grace is without reserve. We truly have the best Daddy ever.

Heavenly Father, thank You for being my Abba, who loves me unconditionally. Let me please You with my life.

> *Knowing therefore the terror of the Lord, we persuade men; but we are made manifest unto God; and I trust also are made manifest in your consciences.*
> —2 Corinthians 5:11

SEPTEMBER 5

We know a day is coming when Jesus will return for His own. We also *know* that on that day many will be left behind. In all likelihood, within our circles of family and friends and acquaintanceship, there are those who have not yet claimed Jesus as Lord. Since we *know* what awaits those who die without Christ, it is our obligation to persuade them otherwise.

Jesus died for you. Will you speak up for Him?

---

*Heavenly Father, thank You for my salvation
and the assurance that my soul is secure.
Please soften the hearts of those who don't yet know You
and let my life be a witness that helps lead them to You.*

Ye offer polluted bread upon mine altar; and ye say, Wherein have we polluted thee? In that ye say, The table of the Lord is contemptible.
—Malachi 1:7

SEPTEMBER 6

Wow, this scripture makes me cringe. Giving the LORD defiled (spoiled, I-don't-want-this-anymore) offerings? What kind of sacrifice is that?

Too often in life we give God less than our best. We give Him our leftover time rather than our first minutes. We only pray after we've sought advice from friends or family or even followers on Facebook. We enter His house with a lackadaisical attitude of "doing our duty" rather than coming in humility and awe with a spirit of worship.

God our Father sacrificed His perfect, sinless Son—the very best!—for us. Should I not offer up my best for him?

Heavenly Father, forgive me for giving You less than my best. May I lay my all in service to You on Your altar.

> *Bring ye all the tithes into the storehouse, that there may be meat in mine house, and prove me now herewith, saith the Lord of hosts, if I will not open you the windows of heaven, and pour you out a blessing, that there shall not be room enough to receive it.*
> —Malachi 3:10

SEPTEMBER 7

I think most Christians are willing to say everything they have is a blessing from God. I think most Christians would also say they believe God will meet their needs. But when it comes to tithing, a lot of Christians are afraid to put that whole ten percent into the offering plate.

I've heard countless testimonies from people who, in faith, honored tithing and discovered their needs were better met on 90% of their income than they'd experienced prior to tithing. Think loaves and fishes. *grin*

"Prove me," the Lord says. His blessings pour over on those who trust Him.

Heavenly Father, thank You for providing for me. If I'm holding something back—whether money, time, or talent— give me the faith to offer it willingly to You.

But God commendeth his love toward us, in that, while we were yet sinners, Christ died for us.
—Romans 5:8

SEPTEMBER 8

Before I earned my college degree, I encountered a catch-22 situation while job-seeking. The companies to which I applied wanted me to have a certain level of experience before they hired me, but the only way I could get experience was by being hired. I wasn't yet "good enough" to become an employee, so I suffered rejection.

But there's no rejection with God! We don't have to have any experience at being good or honorable or truthful or pure to become a part of His family. He loves us right where we are. He sent Jesus to die for us just as we are. All we have to do is come to Him in humility and faith and ask Him to save us, and just like that we're "in." And not temporarily, either—for eternity!

Heavenly Father, thank You for Your love and acceptance. I'm so glad to be part of the family of God!

There is therefore now no condemnation to them which are in Christ Jesus, who walk not after the flesh, but after the Spirit. For the law of the Spirit of life in Christ Jesus hath made me free from the law of sin and death.
—Romans 8:1-2

SEPTEMBER 9

When we are governed by the flesh, we might experience momentary times of pleasure. As a former minister put it, "Sin is fun!" But there is no hope for something more than the *right now*. Death—eternal separation from God—awaits those who serve the flesh.

With Christ, however, death has been conquered. No separation but continual fellowship awaits. The redeemed have hope that extends into eternity, and that realization brings a peace beyond anything the world can offer. Jesus is *life*.

Heavenly Father, thank You for saving my soul.
Thank You for making a place for me in heaven.
Thank You that I am not condemned but am redeemed.

Likewise reckon ye also yourselves to be dead indeed unto sin, but alive unto God through Jesus Christ our Lord.
—Romans 6:11

SEPTEMBER 10

There are lots of wonderful words in the Bible, but I think these from Romans are among my favorites: "reckon ye yourselves to be dead indeed into sin." Dead to sin but alive in Christ—oh, what a beautiful thought! When we accept Jesus as Savior, all sin is washed away. The threat of eternal separation from God is removed. We will be alive forever! We don't have to live mired in regret and guilt and self-recrimination. Salvation...such an incredible gift.

---

*Heavenly Father, thank You for the salvation that gives me life eternal.
I walk in the Light because of Your Son. Hallelujah!*

For when ye were the servants of sin, ye were free from righteousness. What fruit had ye then in those things whereof ye are now ashamed? for the end of those things is death. But now being made free from sin, and become servants to God, ye have your fruit unto holiness, and the end everlasting life. For the wages of sin is death; but the gift of God is eternal life through Jesus Christ our Lord.
—Romans 6:20-23

SEPTEMBER 11

"Holiness" and "eternal life"—aren't those great promises? It can be easy to think, "Well, I'm forgiven, so now I can live how I want to—I'm safe." But how can we be holy when we are still thinking of pleasing self?

Jesus' commitment to us took Him to a painful death on the cross. Shouldn't my commitment to Him be more than accepting His salvation and then returning to the way I lived before? What kind of fruit am I producing? Is my life changed since I asked Jesus to save me from sin's curse?

Heavenly Father, You have saved me.
Please help me live in a way that reflects Your holiness
and bears fruit that furthers Your kingdom.

> *Who, when he came, and had seen the grace of God, was glad, and exhorted them all, that with purpose of heart they would cleave unto the Lord.*
> —Acts 11:23

SEPTEMBER 12

One of the saddest things is when a believer turns away from his or her faith. Often when people turn their backs on God it's because God didn't do what they wanted Him to do. That's actually a little presumptuous. Can the created know better than the Creator what should be done?

God's heart must break when one of His children falls to the pull of the world, but the individual who chooses the world over God also loses. He or she loses peace of mind, security, the strength and comfort God gives, and a sense of belonging. Perhaps this is why Steven encouraged the believers to "cleave unto the Lord" with *all* their hearts. When we let our hearts stray, we lose something precious—intimate fellowship with the Father. Hold tight to your faith! You'll never regret it.

Heavenly Father, You are too good and too wise to make mistakes. Even in times when I don't understand, let me cling to You in faith and trust.

When they heard these things, they held their peace, and glorified God, saying, Then hath God also to the Gentiles granted repentance unto life.
—Acts 11:18

SEPTEMBER 13

Repentance is a word that makes some people uncomfortable because it means admitting they've made a mistake. Remember Fonzie from "Happy Days"? He'd say "I was wr-wr-wr-...not right." Pride keeps us from wanting to admit we were wrong.

Being repentant is humbling, but it is also cleansing. Repentance heals. Repentance leads to everlasting life, leaving us free of the dark mar of sin. Repentance brings us to a place of praise, because it restores our broken fellowship with the Father. If you've committed a wrongdoing, confess it. Repentance leads to restoration, and restoration leads to joy.

*Heavenly Father, thank You for welcoming me
into fellowship with You.
If I've failed You in some way, please forgive me.
May I return to right standing with You.*

Then Peter opened his mouth, and said, Of a truth I perceive that God is no respecter of persons: But in every nation he that feareth him, and worketh righteousness, is accepted with him.
—Acts 10:34-35

SEPTEMBER 14

I spent a lot of years as a 5th grade teacher. Absolutely loved it. Loved the kids. All the kids, although, admittedly, some had a way of weaseling their way into my heart a little deeper than others. However, I did my utmost not to *play* favorites!

God doesn't have favorites. He never shows favoritism. No matter where we've been, no matter what we've done, when we come to Him in faith He holds open His arms and welcomes us in. Remember the song? "The vilest offender who truly believes, that moment from Jesus a pardon receives." No one need ever worry about being good enough or smart enough or whatever enough for God. Salvation is equally available to all.

*Heavenly Father, thank You for Your acceptance
of any sinner who seeks redemption.
When You say "whosoever believes," You mean it.
What a loving God I serve!*

> *There was a certain man in Caesarea called Cornelius, a centurion of the band called the Italian band, A devout man, and one that feared God with all his house, which gave much alms to the people, and prayed to God alway.*
> —Acts 10:1-2

SEPTEMBER 15

This verse, absent of any wise words from Jesus or instruction from one of the disciples, shares something that gives me chills. Do you see what it says? Cornelius and all his household were devout, God-fearing people who prayed to God regularly. What a beautiful testament!

Every day I pray that God will move in the hearts of each of my family members from young to old and that each will choose to serve Him. I would love to have those words describing Cornelius be said about my household someday.

*Heavenly Father, may my entire household
commit to Your service,
and may our faithfulness extend
into the next generations.*

> *Whosoever is born of God doth not commit sin; for his seed remaineth in him: and he cannot sin, because he is born of God.*
> —1 John 3:9

SEPTEMBER 16

I admit...I'm not perfect. (Bet if you're honest, you'll make the same confession.) Here's the thing—as long as we're trapped in a human body, we're going to slip up from time to time. Yes, we will sin. But as we seek God's face and strive to please Him, we won't sin *comfortably*. A Christian's conscience can't stay clear when he or she is openly wallowing in sin. Consequently, we will listen more closely to the Spirit's leading and will sin less frequently.

---

*Heavenly Father, thank You that I am born of You.
Please help me grow in maturity every day.*

For this is the will of God, even your sanctification, that ye should abstain from fornication: That every one of you should know how to possess his vessel in sanctification and honour;
—1 Thessalonians 4:3-4

SEPTEMBER 17

Sexual impurity is kind of an uncomfortable subject, isn't it? But we can't turn on the television, tune the radio, or bring up the Internet without being inundated with sexually immoral images, language, and scenarios. God's plan was for sex to be an expression of love within a committed marriage relationship. With the worldly view of sex being thrown at us from every direction, it's easy to get caught up in seeing it as something recreational or dirty.

As Christians we're to be sanctified. Set apart. Holy. Our bodies are the dwelling place of God's own Spirit! There is no place in the Christian's life for sexual impurity. Guard your thoughts, your actions, and your reactions—let them be a reflection of the One who created you.

Heavenly Father, thank You for Your plan of intimacy within a marriage covenant. Guard my mind and my heart against immorality so I honor You with my body and my behavior.

Furthermore then we beseech you, brethren, and exhort you by the Lord Jesus, that as ye have received of us how ye ought to walk and to please God, so ye would abound more and more.
— 1 Thessalonians 4:1

SEPTEMBER 18

Do you ever get caught up in worrying about what people think about you? I spent a lot of years stressing over what others thought (to the point of physical illness). I regret that worry now. Yes, we should strive to be considerate of others, but the only One we need to truly please is God. When we strive to please Him above all else, we will set an example that some might not appreciate (because it goes against their conscience), but we could very well earn the respect of others by staying true to our convictions. Most of all, we'll please God and grow in our faith, which has an eternal value.

Heavenly Father, for the sake of my Lord Jesus who followed the will of the Father to the cross, may I live my life to please You.

> *Speaking to yourselves in psalms and hymns and spiritual songs, singing and making melody in your heart to the Lord; Giving thanks always for all things unto God and the Father in the name of our Lord Jesus Christ;*
> —Ephesians 5:19b-20

SEPTEMBER 19

Have you ever been stuck in an uncomfortable life-place? Maybe you feel as if you're there right now. Well, here's the way to pass the time while you wait for God's leading: praise Him.

God inhabits praise. When we praise Him, we invite Him to draw near. When He's near, we find peace and comfort and strength to endure whatever situation we are facing. Even when it seems as though the world is falling apart, there is always a reason to thank Him—He save your soul! He never leaves you to face a challenge alone! His love for you is never ending! Praise Him for those truths, and you'll discover the joy of His presence.

---

*Heavenly Father, may I praise You
whether I'm on the mountaintop or in the valley.
Life circumstances change, but You are unchanging,
and I am grateful for Your constancy.*

Wherefore be ye not unwise, but understanding what the will of the Lord is.
—Ephesians 5:17

SEPTEMBER 20

A friend once called me for advice. She said, "I don't know what I'm supposed to do next." My advice was pretty simple: "Then don't move. Not until you have peace about the direction."

Too often we foolishly run ahead of God and then we find ourselves in places we were never meant to be. Sometimes it's a little tough to get out of those situations. So don't run willy-nilly. When you're uncertain, pray, listen, and wait for His leading. His timing is always best, and His direction is always right.

---

*Heavenly Father, thank You for making good plans for me.
Help me seek and follow Your will
so I might be wise.*

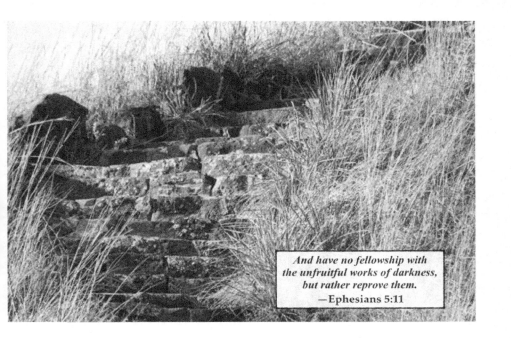

And have no fellowship with the unfruitful works of darkness, but rather reprove them.
—Ephesians 5:11

SEPTEMBER 21

I might be ruffling some feathers with this post, but I have to say it. We sometimes mis-use the scripture about judge not lest ye be judged. No, we can't sit in judgement on others' hearts—that is Jesus's job—but the Lord has given us discernment to judge others' fruits.

If someone is living in a way that is detrimental to him or to others and is in opposition to God's instruction, then it is our responsibility to gently guide them in a better direction. That isn't judging—it's rescuing. Christians should fervently strive to rescue the perishing, or one day we will stand before God and hear Him ask, "Why didn't you try to save My lost?"

---

*Heavenly Father, thank You for saving me.
Please give me the words and the courage
to rescue those trapped in darkness.*

For ye were sometimes darkness, but now are ye light in the Lord: walk as children of light: (For the fruit of the Spirit is in all goodness and righteousness and truth;) Proving what is acceptable unto the Lord.
—Ephesians 5:8-10

SEPTEMBER 22

Many, many years ago, when I was in my early twenties, I heard a minister advise, "Live your life without regrets." I recall thinking then, "How? Tell me how!"

It's pretty hard to live one's life without regrets. We're human. We sometimes mess up, and those mess-ups have unpleasant consequences. But you know, I have no regrets attached to any decision that was made within the bounds of God's instructions. When we strive to live in the light, we have fewer regrets. We might still encounter unpleasantness, because the world doesn't exactly like the Light, but the consequences of others' displeasure cannot bury the self-joy that comes from pleasing the Lord.

*Heavenly Father, help me obey Your precepts,
follow Your Spirit's leading,
and carry no regrets for having failed You.*

Take heed unto thyself, and unto the doctrine; continue in them: for in doing this thou shalt both save thyself, and them that hear thee.
—1 Timothy 4:16

SEPTEMBER 23

There's a parenting tactic that never works. It's the "Do as I say, not as I do" tactic. We can't say, "Be kind," and then speak sharply to a clerk; or say "Don't lie," and then be untruthful to a neighbor. Children will mimic us—it's a given.

We might occasionally fail being a good example to our children, but we never have to worry about God setting a poor example. Thus, as His children, we should do our utmost to mimic the Father. Others are watching our example. When we live as Jesus not only instructed but also lived, we save ourselves, and we have the opportunity to save others as well. I believe that's a "win-win."

Heavenly Father, let me emulate You in how I conduct myself, and let others see You shining through me.

> Now the Spirit speaketh expressly, that in the latter times some shall depart from the faith, giving heed to seducing spirits, and doctrines of devils; Speaking lies in hypocrisy; having their conscience seared with a hot iron;
> —1 Timothy 4:1-2

SEPTEMBER 24

It seems more and more that man has lost his moral compass. Even some who profess Christianity behave in ways that don't reflect our Savior. Staying true to our convictions in this broken world isn't easy, but take heart, Christian—you do not walk this world alone. God's own Spirit indwells you. When in doubt, depend on Him for guidance. The more we listen for His voice and heed it, the less likely it becomes that a worldly influence will pull us astray. We truly have been equipped to emerge holy and blameless. We need only listen and follow.

Heavenly Father, please help me hold firmly to You,
not being swayed by the foolishness of men.
May I be faithful to You and only You.

For there is one God, and one mediator between God and men, the man Christ Jesus; Who gave himself a ransom for all...
—1 Timothy 2:5-6a

SEPTEMBER 25

When my grandson wanted to understand the concept of salvation, I drew him a picture of God and man separated by a great divide called sin. Then I drew a cross like a bridge across the divide and told him Jesus' death on Calvary made it possible for man to draw near to God again, washed free of sin.

Whenever we want to talk to the Father, we can do so through Jesus, our Mediator, the blameless One who gave Himself for all. No man comes to the Father except through the Son. I'm so glad He is available to all who call on His name!

Heavenly Father, thank You that I am able to reach You, thanks to Your Son, the Mediator.

I exhort therefore, that, first of all, supplications, prayers, intercessions, and giving of thanks, be made for all men; For this is good and acceptable in the sight of God our Saviour; Who will have all men to be saved, and to come unto the knowledge of the truth.
— 1 Timothy 2:1, 3-4

SEPTEMBER 26

I've always loved sunbeams—they make me think of when Jesus will return in the clouds. I'm just sure He'll be surrounded by sunbeams, and I'm equally sure the time is drawing nigh.

When I was a little girl, we sang a Sunday school song that started, "Jesus wants me for a sunbeam, To shine for Him each day..." It was written by a man named Nellie Talbot (yes, a man named Nellie!). Even as a kid, I understood why Jesus wanted me to be a sunbeam—you can't help but notice a sunbeam. And when people notice, they have the chance to catch some of the Light. We as believers have a tremendous responsibility to shine for Him. God doesn't want anyone to perish. Are you praying for the lost? Are you living a life that shines Jesus? Shine, child of God, shine!

Heavenly Father, help me shine in such a way that it directs the lost to see Your Son.

But we all, with open face beholding as in a glass the glory of the Lord, are changed into the same image from glory to glory, even as by the Spirit of the Lord.
— 2 Corinthians 3:18

SEPTEMBER 27

Butterflies have to be one of God's most amazing creations. So colorful, so fragile yet so strong. And to think they started out as *worms*.

When God looks at us, does He remember the "worm," or does He only see the beauty of transformation? We were once lost in sin, now cleansed by Jesus' blood. By studying His Word and looking to Him for guidance, we slowly grow into His likeness. Once a lowly sinner, now saved by grace. Amen!

*Heavenly Father, thank You for Your transforming power
that saved me from my life of sin.
Please help me always reflect Your glory.*

For if that which is done away was glorious, much more that which remaineth is glorious.
—2 Corinthians 3:11

SEPTEMBER 28

Moses' face shone with God's glory when he carried the tablets from the mountain. The Law guided the people, and in itself wasn't bad. The problem was no one could follow it completely, so none could be considered righteous. So God, in His infinite love and mercy, sent Jesus. Grace replaced the law. Because of grace, we can live free of sin. What a wonderful, precious gift.

---

*Heavenly Father, You've always wanted the best
for Your children.
Thank You for making a way for us
to be in Your holy presence.
Thank You, Father, for Your grace.*

Now thanks be unto God, which always causeth us to triumph in Christ, and maketh manifest the savour of his knowledge by us in every place. For we are unto God a sweet savour of Christ, in them that are saved, and in them that perish:
—2 Corinthians 2:14-15

SEPTEMBER 29

Yes, I love butterflies. I love their colors, their graceful movements, and the way they gently float on a breeze. It's hard to miss seeing butterflies—they capture our attention with their beauty.

As Christians, our love for others should capture attention as fully as a butterfly's beautiful wings captures attention. We are to be the sweet savour—the pleasant aroma—of Christ. The perishing need the Savior. The way we speak and act could very well be what captures their hearts with a desire for what we have. It isn't easy to be sweet in a "stinky" world, but Christ will help us triumph when we ask for His help.

Heavenly Father, may the aroma of my attitude toward the unsaved be a sweet scent that draws the lost to You.

Forasmuch as ye are manifestly declared to be the epistle of Christ ministered by us, written not with ink, but with the Spirit of the living God; not in tables of stone, but in fleshy tables of the heart.
—2 Corinthians 3:3

SEPTEMBER 30

Meditate on this truth: Christ has engraved His name on our hearts. Celebrate this reality: His Spirit indwells us. We *are* His, and we are *indwelled* by Him!

If we claim the title "Christian," then our love for others should be as evident as letters carved into a stone tablet. Loving isn't always easy, but we don't have to rely on our own power for success. If we let the Spirit lead, then we can display Christ the way we've been called to do.

---

*Heavenly Father, thank You for sealing Your name
on my heart. I am Yours!
Let me live Your love and grace so openly
that no one can deny the difference
You make in a human's life.*

For the Lamb which is in the midst of the throne shall feed them, and shall lead them unto living fountains of waters: and God shall wipe away all tears from their eyes.
—Revelation 7:17

OCTOBER 1

When those of us who have received Jesus as Savior reach the end of our time on this earth, we'll have something special waiting: Eternity with our Shepherd, where no pain or heartache will touch us and no tears will rain from our eyes. I remember so well the final two weeks of my mom's time on earth. She knew her physical body was failing, and as much as she regretted having to leave my dad and the rest of her family, she strained toward heaven. She loved Jesus, and she was eager to see His face, to thank Him for saving her. There was no fear at all—no worry about condemnation, because she knew she had been forgiven.

Seeing her step with confidence and joy toward eternity showed me so clearly that death has no sting for the believer. Believers will reside with the Source of Living Water. What a joy that will be!

---

*Heavenly Father, I'm here on earth
where sadness befalls and tears often flow,
but I know joy awaits me. Thank You for the promise of joy.*

> *Feed the flock of God which is among you, taking the oversight thereof, not by constraint, but willingly; not for filthy lucre, but of a ready mind;*
> —1 Peter 5:2

OCTOBER 2

Christians have a special responsibility toward fellow believers. The Bible directs older Christians to mentor younger ones; it advises younger ones to respect and listen to the elders. A new Christian has a lot to learn, and those who've known the Lord for a longer time can help the new one grow.

We need each other—we need to fellowship together, to support each other, and hold each other accountable. We're family, and families take care of each other.

Heavenly Father, thank You for Your body of believers who support me and help me grow. May I encourage my Christian brothers and sisters by walking rightly with You.

For ye were as sheep going astray; but are now returned unto the Shepherd and Bishop of your souls.
—1 Peter 2:25

OCTOBER 3

When I was six years old, I ran away from home. I was mad at my mom about something—I don't remember what—and I decided I wasn't going to live with her anymore. So I piled what I could in my little red wagon and set off up the street. I didn't make it very far before fear struck: where would I go? what would I do? who would take care of me? I turned around and ran straight to Mom and sobbed out how sorry I was for leaving. She hugged me and told me she was so glad I returned. I learned years later that I hadn't stayed gone long enough for Mom to even miss me. She didn't know I'd left! But still she welcomed me back with a hug and an assurance that I was loved.

No matter how far we stray, we can return to the Shepherd. We'll be welcomed with a hug and an assurance that we are loved. He's the keeper of our souls—not only for now, but for forever.

Heavenly Father, thank You for Your love.
Thank You for welcoming me into Your fold.
May I never intentionally wander away from You.

I am the good shepherd, and know my sheep, and am known of mine.
—John 10:14

OCTOBER 4

There is a tremendous amount of comfort in believing Jesus *knows* me. He understands me completely, nothing I ever do takes Him by surprise, and He is unconditionally committed to being my Shepherd. I am *His*. But there's a flip side to this relationship.

If I claim Him as Shepherd, then it's my responsibility to know Him, too. I need to listen for and heed His voice. I need to follow His directives. How can I accomplish that? Well, by studying His Word; by spending time with Him in prayer; by sitting quietly in His presence. As His sheep, I should emulate my Shepherd.

---

*Heavenly Father, when others look at me,
can they see Who I serve?
Please let them see Jesus in me.*

> *In the body of his flesh through death, to present you holy and unblameable and unreproveable in his sight:*
> —Colossians 1:22

OCTOBER 5

On a grocery store visit, I turned a corner and encountered a roadblock of boxes. I chatted with the stockman while I waited for him to clear the path. When it was open he said, "How you acted just now– patient and kind... You match your shirt." (My shirt had 1 Corinthians 13:4-8 printed on it.) I was so glad I hadn't gotten grumpy about him blocking the aisle! What a horrible witness I would have been!

Because of Jesus, all who claim Him as Lord stand without blemish before Him. We won't be condemned when we reach Heaven's throne. But we should make an effort to stand blameless before man, too. That's how it shows we've been set apart. Holiness has nothing to do with us and *everything* to do with Him.

---

*Heavenly Father, please help me be holy
as You are holy–
set me apart for Your service and witness.*

If ye continue in the faith grounded and settled, and be not moved away from the hope of the gospel, which ye have heard, and which was preached to every creature which is under heaven...
—Colossians 1:23

OCTOBER 6

Do you see security in this scripture? We are free from accusation when we hold to our faith, when we cling to the hope found in the gospel. Our faith in Him should be "grounded and settled"—deeply rooted and unbending. In essence, what we're seeing here is a definition of holiness.

Christianity isn't a religion. It isn't a fad, it isn't something to be sampled, and it isn't a title we wear to stand out. Christianity is a lifestyle of faith rooted in who we believe Jesus to be: our Savior and Redeemer.

Heavenly Father, let me remain deeply rooted and unbending in my faith so others can see the truth that You set a person free.

> *Who is the image of the invisible God, the firstborn of every creature: For by him were all things created, that are in heaven, and that are in earth, visible and invisible, whether they be thrones, or dominions, or principalities, powers: all things were created by him, and for him:*
> —Colossians 1:15-16

OCTOBER 7

Some people have a hard time understanding that all of humanity was created in the image of God. Every time I hear the phrase "white supremacy," I cringe. No one man should hold himself higher than another because of race (or for any other reason). There is only one Supreme Being: the Son, who bears the likeness of the Father. One day He will reign over all nations, and every knee will bow to Him—Jesus, the firstborn over all creation.

Heavenly Father, let me view humanity
through Your eyes of love and compassion.
Let me love unrestrainedly and without bias,
the way You love me.

And he is before all things, and by him all things consist. And he is the head of the body, the church: who is the beginning, the firstborn from the dead; that in all things he might have the preeminence.
—Colossians 1:17-18

OCTOBER 8

The head of the body—now that's supremacy! The title belongs squarely on Jesus. He is before all things. He rules over all things. He holds this world—and us!—together. If we're worshipping (valuing over all) things of this world, we've missed the mark. He is all worthy of worship and praise.

---

*Heavenly Father, thank You for the gift of Your Son,
who reigns triumphant over all.
Let me give Him full control of the reins of my life.*

> *All the paths of the Lord are mercy and truth unto such as keep his covenant and his testimonies.*
> —Psalm 25:10

OCTOBER 9

Who likes landing in trouble? None of us, I'd wager. But even though we don't like being in trouble, we still put ourselves there. It usually happens because we say or do things our conscience advises against. When we get that little catch in our spirit, we need to heed it. Because that's the Holy Spirit saying, "Wait a minute—the Father wouldn't approve of that." When we ignore the Spirit's prompting, the consequences aren't pleasant.

But there's a way to avoid trouble—"keep his covenant and his testimonies." If He instructs us to behave a certain way, we're wise to obey. People will try to draw us off God's pathway, but the Holy Spirit will never lead us astray! Keep His covenant and avoid landing in trouble.

Heavenly Father, this world is fraught with temptations. Please keep my heart centered on You and Your will so I can avoid sin's painful consequences.

Remember, O Lord, thy tender mercies and thy lovingkindnesses; for they have been ever of old.
—Psalm 25:6

OCTOBER 10

I was born and raised in Kansas. Love my endless prairie and expanse of sky that allows a view of sunrises and sunsets. Every summer when I was growing up, my family drove to Colorado and spent a week in the mountains. That's how I learned to love mountains. Tall. Majestic. Permanent. They remind me of my Creator.

God's love for you was in place before the mountains were constructed by His hand. The Alpha and Omega loves you. Loves you with a deeper compassion and faithfulness than anyone can fathom. From age to age, He is the same: your Savior, your Redeemer, your Lord.

---

*Heavenly Father, Your love for me
is as immovable as a mountain.
Thank You for choosing me to be Yours.*

> *Lead me in thy truth, and teach me: for thou art the God of my salvation; on thee do I wait all the day.*
> —Psalm 25:5

OCTOBER 11

My favorite line in this scripture is "on thee I do wait all the day." Jesus is coming again! I catch myself looking to the clouds in anticipation. While we wait, no matter what happens in this life, we are *never* without hope because we know we have a place prepared for us in heaven. In the meantime, we have the joy of His presence, the strength of His hand, and the peace of His spirit.

Heavenly Father, You are my Hope!
Not only for today, but for all of my tomorrows
and into eternity.

That as sin hath reigned unto death, even so might grace reign through righteousness unto eternal life by Jesus Christ our Lord.
—Romans 5:21

OCTOBER 12

After my mother graduated to heaven, I inherited her Bible. She'd only written one thing in it: her favorite verse, 1 Corinthians 1:13, "No temptation has overtaken you except what is common to mankind. And God is faithful; he will not let you be tempted beyond what you can bear." I was surprised by her choice because, honestly, my mama was one of the most faithful saints I'd ever known. I couldn't imagine her battling temptation. But then it occurred to me she was faithful because she consistently trusted God to help her overcome temptation.

Sin needn't reign in us when we lean into His strength. And when we enter Glory, no more will sin tease and tempt—righteousness will be our robe. Amen!

Heavenly Father, thank You for the ability to overcome temptation so sin doesn't rule in me. Thank You for the victory You give us through Jesus.

For as by one man's disobedience many were made sinners, so by the obedience of one shall many be made righteous.
—Romans 5:19

OCTOBER 13

I used to have a poster of a sad-looking puppy with the caption, "Nobody's perfect." So very true. We're trapped down here in human bodies. Our spirits are so often willing, but our flesh is weak. We mess up. In other words, we sin. And like Adam and Eve, when we sin, we want to point a finger of blame at someone else.

But we should avoid the world's penchant for blaming somebody else or making excuses. Instead, we should tell God we're sorry. Because of Jesus's perfect life and His death on the cross, we can be be forgiven. Wiped clean. Made righteous again. What a wonderful gift is forgiveness.

Heavenly Father, thank You for forgiving me when I fall.
Thank You for making me clean in Your sight.
Help me walk righteously and avoid the pitfalls of sin.

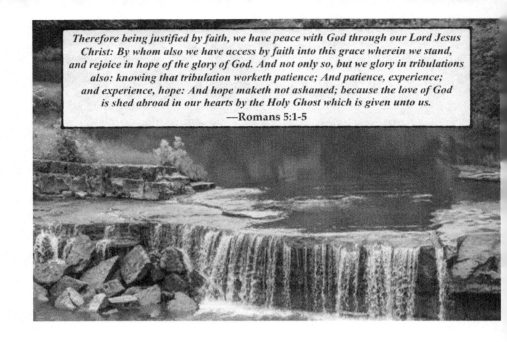

Therefore being justified by faith, we have peace with God through our Lord Jesus Christ: By whom also we have access by faith into this grace wherein we stand, and rejoice in hope of the glory of God. And not only so, but we glory in tribulations also: knowing that tribulation worketh patience; And patience, experience; and experience, hope: And hope maketh not ashamed; because the love of God is shed abroad in our hearts by the Holy Ghost which is given unto us.
—Romans 5:1-5

OCTOBER 14

It's easy to rejoice when things are going well, but not so easy when life is tough. But here we so clearly see the value of conflict. Walking through a trial is an exercise in patience and perseverance—both very worthwhile qualities to nurture. The experience strengthens our dependence on and our walk with God. And the positive end result in times of suffering: it leads to *hope*.

In the midst of the conflict, we aren't alone. The Holy Spirit comforts us, strengthens us, and guides us. So rejoice, dear Christian! We are never without hope.

*Heavenly Father, You are the Author of Hope.
Thank You for bestowing it on me!*

If we confess our sins, he is faithful and just to forgive us our sins, and to cleanse us from all unrighteousness.
—1 John 1:9

OCTOBER 15

This scripture is probably underlined in your Bible. Am I right? It's such a beautiful verse despite the ugly "sin" reference. There is no sin too big that God won't forgive it. There is no stain so dark God can't purify it. The sad part is how so many want to hold on to their sins—keep them secret in the hope "no one will know," and by so doing live with a feeling of shame or helplessness or despair that colors every aspect of their lives and robs them of joy.

Christians aren't meant to be joyless. God is so faithful, so just, and so compassionate. We can go to Him with any and all of our "broken toys," and He will restore them...and us!...to wholeness.

Heavenly Father, may I never try to hide my sins from You but confess them openly and with sincere repentance.

This then is the message which we have heard of him, and declare unto you, that God is light, and in him is no darkness at all. If we say that we have fellowship with him, and walk in darkness, we lie, and do not practice the truth:
—1 John 1:5b-6

OCTOBER 16

There are a lot of people who use the term "Christian" loosely. They call themselves a Christian because they live in America, or because Grandpa was a preacher, or because Mom and Dad took them to church. But "Christian" isn't a title. It's a lifestyle born of relationship. If we truly are Christians, it should show in the way we speak, the way we treat others, the very way we live. Darkness (i.e., the way of the world) has no place in a true Christian's life.

Every now and then it's good to examine oneself and ask God to reveal any darkness that needs to be eradicated. Those of us who call Him Father don't have room in our hearts for elements of darkness.

*Heavenly Father, thank You for redeeming me.
If there is any way within me that doesn't show Your Light,
please diminish it and let me shine only You.*

(For the life was manifested, and we have seen it, and bear witness, and shew unto you that eternal life, which was with the Father, and was manifested unto us;)
—1 John 1:2

OCTOBER 17

Jesus gave His followers a very distinct assignment: Go into all the world and preach the gospel to every nation. Those things which they had seen—His miracles, His death and resurrection—were to be proclaimed again and again and again.

Those who *know* the difference He makes are commanded to share the truth with those who do not yet know. The Life appeared! He brought eternal life! We have met Him and accepted Him and discovered the difference He makes! To whom will you proclaim Him today?

---

*Heavenly Father, You have changed and enriched my life.
Let me speak of Your goodness and grace
in both my words and my walk.*

O LORD, truly I am thy servant
—Psalm 116:16a

OCTOBER 18

Truly I am thy servant. Aren't those weighty words? Someone who lives for Him first and self second is His servant. Someone who strives to walk in obedience to His guidance rather than following his own behavioral compass is His servant. Are His servants perfect? No, but they are holy–set apart from the world for His purposes. Being His servant is better than any other position in the world.

It's one thing to ask Jesus to be our Savior; it's another to truly make Him Lord of our life. But oh, the change that comes when we commit ourselves fully to Him. May this be our heartfelt prayer of submission:

Heavenly Father, let me be Thy servant.

Precious in the sight of the Lord is the death of his saints.
—Psalm 116:15

OCTOBER 19

None of us like to think about death, but it's inevitable for all of us (unless the Lord comes first). While I'd rather not dwell on death, I do occasionally consider what kind of legacy I'm leaving. Because we all make an impact on this earth, for good or for not so good. The best legacy is one of faith, of honoring God with the whole heart.

When we reach heaven's gate, God will look in His Book of Life. If we've acknowledged Jesus as Savior and Lord, God will swing wide the gate and say, "Come in, my child!" And all of heaven will rejoice at our arrival.

Heavenly Father, one day I will stand in Your presence. Until that day, let me live for You and leave behind footprints of faithfulness for others to follow.

> *Thine eyes did see my substance, yet being unperfect; and in thy book all my members were written, which in continuance were fashioned, when as yet there was none of them. How precious also are thy thoughts unto me, O God! how great is the sum of them! If I should count them, they are more in number than the sand: when I awake, I am still with thee.*
> —Psalm 139:16-18

OCTOBER 20

Beautiful words. Beautiful, beautiful words rich with meaning... God knew the number of your days even before one of them came to be. He thinks of you. He thinks of you so frequently, the thoughts can't even be counted because they outnumber the grains of sand. Do you see how much God anticipated your arrival? How much you are loved? You are special and important to God the Father. You are loved with an everlasting love.

Spend some time today reflecting on the Father's great love for you.

Heavenly Father, thank You for loving me with a love beyond comprehension.

> *Search me, O God, and know my heart: try me, and know my thoughts: And see if there be any wicked way in me, and lead me in the way everlasting.*
> —Psalm 139:23-24

OCTOBER 21

*I*n September of 2004, I met with a woman named Brandilyn in a room which had been set aside for conference attendees to use as a prayer closet. On that day, God revealed the emotional source of my six chronic illnesses, and He stripped me of the burden of shame. I was healed that day. At the end of her prayer, Brandilyn told me something I've never forgotten: "Kim, you've developed a habit of worry. He'll help you, but you're going to have to break that. God didn't heal your habit."

Harmful habits, such as a penchant for constant worry, become so ingrained in our lives that we can lose the ability to see them as harmful. Worry was commonplace for me, but not until Brandilyn's straightforward comment did I realize what my habit was telling God: I don't trust You. I'm so grateful for her honesty, and I'm grateful that I have learned to trust in place of worry. How do I know? My stomach doesn't hurt anymore. He not only healed me, He revealed a "wicked way" and then lovingly led me away from it.

Use today's scripture as your prayer. Your life will be enriched if you open your heart to His leading.

Little children, let no man deceive you: he that doeth righteousness is righteous, even as he is righteous.
—1 John 3:7

OCTOBER 22

Until Jesus returns or death claims our bodies, we're stuck down here. While we are, we must guard our hearts. This world will pull at us with countless temptations. Stand firm, dear Christian. Don't give the devil a victory by being led astray. A wonderful reward awaits us in Heaven—something so much better than anything this world can offer. Be righteous, as Jesus showed us to live.

Heavenly Father, prevent my heart from being swayed by deception. Let me truly be righteous in Your sight.

Behold, what manner love the Father hath bestowed upon us, that we should be called the sons of God: therefore the world knoweth us not, because it knew him not.
—1 John 3:1

OCTOBER 23

My dad isn't a terribly demonstrative person. Because he didn't hear the words "I love you" when he was growing up (his mother died when he was very young and his father wasn't a loving man), he has a hard time saying those words. Even so, I've never doubted his love for me. He's shown it in the way he's always taken care of me. And I've always tried to behave in a way that wouldn't bring him grief.

As much as Daddy loves me, God loves me more. And I love Him as a patient, attentive, ever-present Father. If we love and respect Him, we will live in a way that doesn't disappoint Him. When people look at me, will they know I'm God's girl? I sure hope so.

*Heavenly Father, being Your child is my greatest privilege and my awesome responsibility.
May I bring You joy as I strive to honor You.*

And that ye study to be quiet, and to do your own business, and to work with your own hands, as we commanded you; That ye may walk honestly toward them that are without, and that ye may have lack of nothing.
—1 Thessalonians 4:11-12

OCTOBER 24

Does this scripture make you think of the Old Order religious groups? It's actually pretty good advice. If we keep our hands occupied doing good works, our minds will be too focused on our own behavior to gossip about someone else's actions. *grin*

Actually, the most important part of the verse, in my opinion, is *why* we should live a quiet life, not stirring up conflict or behaving in a manner that calls attention to self. We want to be respected because we are a representation of God here on earth. Our lives should be a reflection of the Savior, who strove to point everyone's eyes heavenward to the Father.

Heavenly Father, keep my eyes and my focus on You, and let the work of my hands bring You glory.

Gracious is the Lord, and righteous; yea, our God is merciful.
—Psalm 116:5

OCTOBER 25

Consider the author of Psalm 116, King David. He was one of the Lord's servants, but he wasn't perfect. He committed adultery and even murder! Yet He wrote, "...God is full of compassion." David had experienced God's unconditional love and forgiveness. That same gracious compassion is offered to each of us, but I think we need to exercise caution about taking advantage of God's willingness to forgive any sin. Instead of doing whatever we want to because "God loves me anyway," we should try to live in a way that shows respect to God and His expectations for believers. Yes, He always loves, but how we pierce Him when we deliberately sin against Him.

Heavenly Father, I love You.
Let me never take Your compassion for granted,
but let me walk in righteousness.

For in him we live, and move, and have our being...
—Acts 17:28a

OCTOBER 26

My cats love to watch the "birdies" that congregate around the bird feeder in our back yard. I like watching them, too. They are so fascinating! So delicate in appearance, yet strong enough to fly thousands of miles or progress against a stout wind. God built so many uniquenesses into the various creatures on this earth. And He built uniquenesses in us, too.

He gave us emotions, and a will, and abilities intended to bring us satisfaction. More than that, He put His breath of life into us. We are His most precious creation because we carry His image. In Him we have our being. We are treasured and loved.

Heavenly Father, thank You for the gifts You give.
Mostly, thank You for life and life abundant
from the saving grace found in Jesus Christ.

And hath made of one blood all nations of men for to dwell on all the face of the earth, and hath determined the times before appointed, and the bounds of their habitation; That they should seek the Lord, if haply they might feel after him, and find him, though he be not far from every one of us:
—Acts 17:26-27

OCTOBER 27

For reasons I don't understand, I've always loved fences. I take pictures of them wherever I travel, and one in Miami, Florida, was so unique in its construction. At first glance, I thought it was concrete, but when I got close I realized it was made of rocks. Tiny crustaceans and crystals were embedded in the coral-like stones.

The evidence of past life made me think of all the generations of people who have lived before me. The details gave me a glimpse of God's creation. As I brushed my fingers over the rocks and the curled shells from sea snails or clams, I felt close to the Maker of the universe. He's never far away. All we have to do is stretch out our hand…and He is there.

Heavenly Father, thank You for the reminders of Your greatness that we find when we take the time to look. Thank You for Your presence.

> God that made the world and all things therein, seeing that he is Lord of heaven and earth, dwelleth not in temples made with hands;
> —Acts 17:24

OCTOBER 28

One of the best aspects of Christianity is that we don't have to visit a "place" to access our God. He is always available, because He lives within us in the form of the Holy Spirit. Think about this…the God who created everything in the expansive heavens and on this meticulously crafted earth chooses to live in you! If that doesn't make you feel special, I don't know what will.

Heavenly Father, of all the places You could be,
You chose to be with me.
Thank You. Thank You.

> *But when the Comforter is come, whom I will send unto you from the Father, even the Spirit of truth, which proceedeth from the Father, he shall testify of me: And ye also shall bear witness, because ye have been with me from the beginning.*
> —John 15:26-27

OCTOBER 29

God is such a compassionate father. He gave us a piece of Himself with the indwelling of the Holy Spirit. Because of His presence, we are never alone. We never have to stand on our own feeble strength. We have a ready moral compass, advisor, and life guide! And He gives us the words we need to testify for Jesus Christ.

Please don't shrink in shame or embarrassment when the chance to share the gift of salvation arises. Our Jesus suffered public humiliation for us and prepared a place for us in Heaven. Let's be bold enough to speak for Him on this earth.

---

*Heavenly Father, the willing sacrifice Jesus made
is beyond anything most can imagine.
Let me testify to what He did for me
and let all come to receive Him as Lord.*

If the world hate you, ye know that it hated me before it hated you. If ye were of the world, the world would love his own: but because ye are not of the world, but I have chosen you out of the world, therefore the world hateth you.
—John 15:18-19

OCTOBER 30

Years ago a friend was facing more trials that she could count—health challenges, broken relationships, financial hardship... One attack after another. All I could think was, "She must be doing something right to warrant this much attention from the deceiver."

When we choose to follow Jesus, we can expect trials. Our spirit and the world's spirit will be at war. But stand firm! We've been *chosen* to be children of God. Our eternal reward awaits us. What He gives is so much better than anything this world can offer.

---

*Heavenly Father, when hardships come,
as I know they will,
let me stand strong in You.*

*I am the vine,
ye are the branches:
He that abideth in me,
and I in him,
the same bringeth forth
much fruit: ... Herein is
my Father glorified,
that ye bear much fruit;
so shall ye be my disciples.*
—John 15:5, 8

OCTOBER 31

How will others know we are Christians unless our words and actions validate it? A Bible study leader at church once shared that our status as God's children defines our values, and our values drive our behavior. Do you see the connection?

We glorify our Father when we behave in a way that points others to Him. We can't do it on our own. We stumble and fall and fail in our own strength. But He can and will work in us and through us when we stay close to Him.

*Heavenly Father, a closer walk with You is what I want.
Draw me near and let me glorify You.*

I am the true vine, and my Father is the husbandman. Every branch in me that beareth not fruit he taketh away: and every branch that beareth fruit, he purgeth it, that it may bring forth more fruit. Now ye are clean through the word which I have spoken unto you. Abide in me, and I in you. As the branch cannot bear fruit of itself, except it abide in the vine; no more can ye, except ye abide in me.
—John 15:1-4

NOVEMBER 1

When we interact with others, do they see love, joy, peace, patience, kindness, goodness, faithfulness, gentleness, and self-control? These are the fruits produced by a person in tune with the Holy Spirit. We cannot bear those kinds of fruits on our own. Human nature gets in the way. But we can be successful by following Jesus's example. When we know Him, when we study His Word, when we spend time with Him in prayer, when we seek to do His will, then these wonderful fruits take root in our hearts and abide in us as they do in Him. It's so simple: if we are His, it will show in our fruit.

Heavenly Father, thank You for caring enough to work in and through me to bring about the kind of fruit that benefits Your kingdom and grows Your child in faith.

> *I know both how to be abased,
> and I know how to abound:
> every where and in all things
> I am instructed both to be full
> and to be hungry,
> both to abound and to suffer need.
> I can do all things through Christ
> which strengtheneth me.*
> —Philippians 4:12-13

NOVEMBER 2

Do you ever feel as if you can't take one more step? Right now within my circle of acquaintanceship I can count more than a dozen people facing challenging situations. But you know what? I can also give you testimony after testimony how those people are enduring because they've learned to lean into Jesus's strength rather than depending on their own.

There is a secret to living contentedly: I can do all this through *Him* who gives me strength.

---

*Heavenly Father, in moments when I am overwhelmed
and at my weakest, thank You for Your sustaining strength.
Let me find my contentment in knowing You.*

> Behold, what manner of love the Father hath bestowed upon us, that we should be called the sons of God: therefore the world knoweth us not, because it knew him not.
> —1 John 3:1c

NOVEMBER 3

It's tough to be a Christian sometimes (just read the news…). People aren't always kind or understanding or "tolerant." Sometimes they outright reject us because we don't participate in activities the world views as acceptable. But should the world's view change our moral compass? Absolutely not!

We are *in* this world, but as His children, we aren't *of* it. Continue to walk in His ways. Continue to speak His truth. Yes, there will be some who respond negatively to our faith. That's just the way it will be. But there are others who might be changed because we stood firm. Remember Philippians 4:13—we can stay faithful against adversity because of His strength. Victory is ours.

Heavenly Father, I am Yours.
Being known by You is better than being accepted by the world.
Let me stand firm in Your precepts.

> *For God hath not called us unto uncleanness, but unto holiness. He therefore that despiseth, despiseth not man, but God, who hath also given unto us his holy Spirit.*
> —1 Thessalonians 4:7-8

NOVEMBER 4

Christians, when we knowingly and intentionally wallow in the world's practices, we're doing so much more than satisfying flesh or "tripping" or "being human." We are rejecting God's instruction.

The same God who sent Jesus into the world to die for our sins calls us to holiness—a holiness made possible by Jesus' sacrifice. Do we really want to reject God? Do we want to ignore the Holy Spirit's prompting for a few minutes of worldly pleasure? God gave us so much. The least we can give Him is our dedication.

---

*Heavenly Father, please forgive my failings
and keep me steady in following You.
You hold the keys to true life.*

Not that I speak in respect of want: for I have learned, in whatsoever state I am, therewith to be content.
—Philippians 4:11

NOVEMBER 5

The Hubs and I are John Wayne fans. One of our favorite movies is "True Grit." At one point, young Maddie Ross says, "I've had enough, and enough is as good as a feast." I've thought about that line so many times when tempted to be jealous of someone. God gives me enough. Not only that, *He* is my Enough. When I consider how my needs are met, how blessed I am, contentment wells inside of me. Regardless of the circumstance, I have God. And He is enough.

---

*Heavenly Father, thank You for filling me
and completing me.
A relationship with You is my enough.*

Finally, brethren, whatsoever things are true, whatsoever things are honest, whatsoever things are just, whatsoever things are pure, whatsoever things are lovely, whatsoever things are of good report; if there be any virtue, and if there be any praise, think on these things. …and the God of peace shall be with you.
—Philippians 4:8-9

NOVEMBER 6

Nutritionists say "You are what you eat." It's true of other things, too. Whatever we take in affects us. If we surround ourselves with negative (i.e., spiritually unwise) influences, we will end up becoming negative, too. God advises us to keep our focus on those things that promote His Kingdom.

So how do we focus on the true, just, pure, lovely, and praiseworthy? We'll find perfect peace when our minds are stayed (fixed) on Him. We should be aware of what's happening in our world, but we don't have to dwell on it or let it eat at us. If we turn our worries and concerns over to Him, trusting Him to work His will, then we can move forward in confidence instead of fear. Reflecting on God's power and goodness is our surest path to inner peace.

Heavenly Father, help me remember that You are more powerful than any world source. Let my mind find peace in Your truths.

> ...the peace of God, which passeth all understanding, shall keep your hearts and minds through Christ Jesus.
> —Philippians 4:7

NOVEMBER 7

Worrying was a hard thing for me to overcome. But on September 20, 2004, I made a commitment to place my concerns in His hands rather than stewing. And you know what? I haven't had a stomach ulcer since. I wish I'd done better about praying—thanking Him for His presence in the past and trusting Him to guide me in the future—when I was younger. Maybe I could have avoided those ulcers! But I have learned there is peace in trusting.

I don't always understand why things happen the way they do, but my faith is based on knowing that He knows. And that is enough.

---

*Heavenly Father, let me praise You
on the mountaintops and in the darkest valleys,
knowing that wherever I am, You are there.*

...being predestinated according to the purpose of him who worketh all things after the counsel of his own will:
—Ephesians 1:11b

NOVEMBER 8

One of my favorite verses comes from Jeremiah 29—God makes plans for us that are intended to give us hope. His plans hold a specific purpose: to bring us joy and give Him glory.

We travel lots of different roads in this world. Much of the time, we can't see what waits around the bend. Sometimes that's a little scary! But God sees. He knows. And we can trust Him to already be waiting around that bend, ready to bestow the strength, discernment, and peace we'll need to continue the pathway. We can always trust His plans.

Heavenly Father, there is much uncertainty in this world.
But there is no uncertainty with You.
You are my security and strength.

> *Wherein he hath abounded toward us in all wisdom and prudence;*
> —Ephesians 1:8

NOVEMBER 9

So often I feel clueless. I don't understand why things happen the way they do, and I aim endless questions at my Father-God. (It's okay to question Him. He knows our secret thoughts anyway, so why not be open and honest with Him? He can take it.)

Sometimes, as a mom, I didn't explain the reasons for decisions to my children; I told them I was Mom and they needed to trust my judgment. I think God brings us to that place of trust and wisdom, too. We don't have to know "why" if we believe God our Father knows best. Finding that place of trust is a great place to be.

Heavenly Father, when I don't understand the why, help me rest in who You are.

> *To the praise of the glory of his grace, wherein he hath made us accepted in the beloved.*
> —Ephesians 1:6

NOVEMBER 10

I was a painfully shy child who moved a lot. I rarely felt as if I fit in at school or in the neighborhood. But the one place I always fit was church. Particularly during hymn-singing. Adding my voice to others', joining in that four-part harmony, gave me a sense of belonging that still warms me in remembrance today.

Have you praised God for the wonderful gift of grace He pours on us? Have you thanked Him for making You part of the family of God? Christians always have a reason for a joyous heart. No circumstance or life happening can rob us of His love or steal us away from Him. So praise Him!

Heavenly Father, thank You for seeing me as Your beloved. Thank You that I always "fit" with You.

> *Be not forgetful to entertain strangers: for thereby some have entertained angels unawares.*
> —Hebrews 13:2

NOVEMBER 11

"To err on the side of kindness is seldom an error." This statement was made by a woman named Liz Armbruster. That name might not be familiar to you, but it was a mantra by which a more familiar woman lived. Her name was Mother Teresa, and she spent her life trying to love the way Jesus loved.

It's so easy to go about our business, wrapped up in our own little worlds, oblivious to the needs around us. How about asking God to let us look at others the way He does? He'll open our eyes (and our hearts) and give us the means to bring His love to the hurting, needy hearts around us. Who knows? We might even minister to an angel unaware.

Heavenly Father, give me Your eyes and Your heart—
let me see and respond to the hurting souls I encounter
in a way that brings glory to Your name.

God, who at sundry times and in divers manners spake in time past unto the fathers by the prophets, Hath in these last days spoken unto us by his Son...
—Hebrews 1:1-2a

NOVEMBER 12

God has always spoken to His children. Creation sings His praise. He used signs and miracles to point to Himself. He spoke through prophets and through His written, inspired Word. But then came Jesus, and now God speaks to us through His Son.

We are a blessed generation! No more burning a sacrifice on an altar as a sign of remorse—we can speak to the Father through the Son. Salvation and eternal hope arrived in Jesus Christ, our personal Lord and Savior.

Heavenly Father, thank You for wanting a relationship with me. Thank You for listening to me and for speaking to me. May I always heed Your voice.

> The grass withereth,
> the flower fadeth:
> but the word
> of our God
> shall stand for ever.
> —Isaiah 40:8

NOVEMBER 13

Aren't you thankful that in a world that is so rapidly changing (technology, weather, morals, education, values...) there is one stable: God's Word. It never goes out of style, never wavers in its expectations, never becomes obsolete. The world is trying so hard to rewrite the Bible to match today's standards of morality, but it won't work. The Bible isn't meant to be changed; it's meant to change you.

Need stability? Open the Bible...it provides a solid base on which we can always securely stand.

---

*Heavenly Father, thank You for Your Word,
which is always applicable, always wise, always good.
Let me obey it always in all ways.*

Blessed be the God and Father of our Lord Jesus Christ, which according to his abundant mercy hath begotten us again unto a lively hope by the resurrection of Jesus Christ from the dead
—1 Peter 1:3

NOVEMBER 14

What an interesting turn of phrase: a lively hope. Not a maybe hope. Not something we say with a sigh or with half-hearted enthusiasm. Lively hope–living hope, exciting hope, never-ending hope.

Praise Him for the hope He has given us! Jesus coming to earth, sacrificing Himself at Calvary, and conquering death have paved the way for each of us to *know God intimately*. To have a *personal relationship* with God the Father. That's something to get "lively" about.

---

*Heavenly Father, thank You for the hope of heaven
and the hope of Your presence on earth
and the hope of knowing I am ever Yours.
Let me live this hope so enthusiastically it trickles over
and spills out on all who know me.*

> *Wherefore, my dearly beloved, flee from idolatry.*
> —1 Corinthians 10:14

NOVEMBER 15

Chances are none of us have little brass or gold idols to which we bow down and worship, but there are other means of "idolatry" in our lives. Anything that comes before God or interferes with our relationship with Him can be considered an idol.

It's a good idea for the Christian to take stock now and then and see if activities or the pursuit of belongings is becoming so important we neglect our time with our Father. If so, flee! He is our greatest satisfaction, so keep Him "front and center."

Heavenly Father, if there is anything taking control of me that pushes You to the side, rid me of it. Fill me with You.

> *Having predestinated us unto the adoption of children by Jesus Christ to himself, according to the good pleasure of his will*
> —Ephesians 1:5

NOVEMBER 16

Have you ever felt like singing that children's song, "Nobody likes me, everybody hates me, I think I'll go eat worms..."? It's a pretty silly song, but the feeling of being unloved is far from funny. My dad lost his mom when he was very young. After her death, no one told him they loved him. He felt in the way and unwanted. But shortly before his mother's death, he had knelt in church and asked Jesus into his heart. When he started feeling unloved by the people in his life, he remembered that he was loved by God, and that recognition sustained him through a painful childhood.

Guess what? *You* are loved. Long, long ago God made the way for you to become an adopted child in His family. It gives Him pleasure to call you "son" or "daughter." So if you're feeling unloved today, don't go eat worms. *smile* Bask in the reality that *you are loved* with an eternal love by the Maker of the heavens and the earth. Yes, you *are* loved.

---

*Heavenly Father, thank You for wanting me,
for choosing me, and for loving me forever.*

But the God of all grace, who hath called us unto his eternal glory by Christ Jesus, after that ye have suffered a while, make you perfect, stablish, strengthen, settle you.
—1 Peter 5:10

NOVEMBER 17

Temptations will come. We'll stumble and fall. We'll often fail. We're trapped in human skin with human thoughts and feeling and emotions, and sometimes they're gonna win. *But take heart.* God's grace is always available. He will renew us when we turn to Him, and we can be firm and steadfast when we stand in *His* strength.

Heavenly Father, thank You for Your strength.
Guard my feet and keep me on Your pathway.

> *Be sober, be vigilant; because your adversary the devil, as a roaring lion, walketh about, seeking whom he may devour: Whom resist stedfast in the faith, knowing that the same afflictions are accomplished in your brethren that are in the world.*
> —1 Peter 5:8-9

NOVEMBER 18

One of the biggest misconceptions about Christianity is that Christians will never have anything bad happen to them. The truth is, Christians *will* be attacked with temptation and discouragement. They'll face fiery trials and outright persecution—often more so than non-Christians. Why? Because the devil doesn't want anyone sold out for Christ. When we make an open commitment to serve Him, we put ourselves directly in opposition to the enemy.

But here's the good news: the evil one can torment us, but he can't defeat us. Jesus already holds the victory!

Heavenly Father, when trials and temptations come my way, help me view them as a means of growing deeper in faith. May I be a living example of the difference You make in a human's heart and life.

Casting all your care upon him; for he careth for you.
—1 Peter 5:7

NOVEMBER 19

God cares. He cares even more than your mom or your sister or your closest friend cares. When we're burdened or upset, our first inclination is to talk to someone close to us, and we usually choose someone in human skin. There's nothing wrong with that unless we're using the person as replacement for the One who owns our heart.

No other person, no matter how much they love you or might want to help, can love bigger or do more than God. If we want true peace, if we want solutions, if we want someone who truly understands every part of why we are troubled, then there's only one place to go: to the Father. Take your concerns and hurts to Him. He's ready to listen.

---

*Heavenly Father, forgive me for looking past You
and using others to meet my emotional needs.
You are the one who knows me best.
Thank You for caring so deeply for me.*

> *Humble yourselves therefore under the mighty hand of God, that he may exalt you in due time:*
> —1 Peter 5:6

NOVEMBER 20

Somehow being in a hopeless pit makes us realize how much we need a Savior. Human pride can really trip us up, making us think we can handle things all on our own. When we come to the realization that in ourselves we are weak and unable, then God can work in us and through us to bring us to victory. Are you struggling today? Bow to Him and allow His strength to bolster you.

---

*Heavenly Father, You are my Sustainer when I am spent.
Let me lean into Your strength, and when I emerge triumphant,
may the glory for the victory be Yours alone.*

Likewise, ye younger, submit yourselves unto the elder. Yea, all of you be subject one to another, and be clothed with humility: for God resisteth the proud, and giveth grace to the humble.
—1 Peter 5:5

NOVEMBER 21

Humility isn't a sense of self-denigration but more of self-awareness. He's God; we aren't. We aren't all-knowing and all-powerful, but we know Who is. Therefore, we walk in humility before Him and before those who are older and wiser in the faith.

No one really likes the word "submit," because pride prevents us from wanting to be "below" someone else. But can we really handle all of life on our own? Not successfully. When we come to the realization that in ourselves we are weak and unable, then God can work in us and through us to bring us to victory.

Heavenly Father, build in me a heart of humility that listens and responds to Your Spirit's leading.

He restoreth my soul...
—Psalm 23:3a

NOVEMBER 22

When you come to the end of yourself—when you realize you cannot handle things on your own—and you turn to Him, He strengthens you.

When you admit your wrongdoings, He forgives you.

When you fall and feel scuffed and bruised and broken, He picks you up.

He is your Restorer.

Heavenly Father, You are the restorer of my soul.
Thank You for loving me enough to be my Restorer.

He maketh me to lie down in green pastures...
—Psalm 23:2a

NOVEMBER 23

I researched sheep a few years ago, and I was stunned to discover they will not rest unless directed to do so. They will actually walk themselves to death! What a metaphor for life I see in that little tidbit of information.

We can bring spiritual death upon ourselves when we don't take the time to refresh ourselves with worship and praise. God knew we'd need that time of refreshment when He directed us to keep the Sabbath holy. Take time for Him—your spirit (and your physical body!) will thank you for it.

Heavenly Father, in this hurry-up and oh-so-busy world, it can be hard to carve out time for spiritual rest. Remind me how much I need that blessed time with You.

*The LORD is my shepherd;
I shall not want.*
—Psalm 23:1

NOVEMBER 24

I've always loved thinking of Jesus as the Good Shepherd. The shepherd guides the sheep, sees to their needs, protects them even to the point of laying down his life for his sheep. To know that I have a Savior who is so attentive, so giving, so compassionate brings a joy that satisfies my deepest longings. I am His, which means I have everything I need.

---

*Heavenly Father, when human wants begin to create dissatisfaction within my heart, remind me that You are my Everything.
In You, I am complete.*

> *For the invisible things of him from the creation of the world are clearly seen, being understood by the things that are made, even his eternal power and Godhead; so that they are without excuse:*
> —Romans 1:20

NOVEMBER 25

When I taught history, I was always amazed how every culture had its god. Men have an inborn need for a Creator. So how can people scoff at the idea of God? They're denying a piece of themselves by claiming there is no Creator, and they're blaspheming God Himself.

God has deliberately displayed His power and glory and beauty in this world. The proof of His creative hand is everywhere we look! There is no excuse for saying, "There is no God." He hung the moon and stars in the sky so men would look up and seek Him. He isn't just *a* god—He is God. And He reigns forever!

Heavenly Father, You created this world, and You created me. May my life give credence to Your presence.

beloved of God, called to be saints...
—Romans 1:7b

NOVEMBER 26

What beautiful words: You are God's beloved! You've been set apart by Him. You've been set apart *for* Him. He has a purpose for your life—to be holy and to walk in confidence and joy with Him. How can we show our appreciation for the unconditional, never-ending, all-encompassing love He bestows on us? It's very simple: Live for Him.

Heavenly Father, I am Your beloved
and You are my Father.
I am never purposeless or useless.
Thank You for calling me.

> *Thine eyes did see my substance,
> yet being unperfect; and in thy book
> all my members were written,
> which in continuance were fashioned,
> when as yet there was none of them.*
> —Psalm 139:16

NOVEMBER 27

Psalm 139 is a great go-to chapter when you're feeling a little down on yourself. (Hey, it happens to all of us from time to time.) But these words—that God saw you before you were born, that He fashioned you together, that He laid out a plan for your life—tells you so clearly that He cares deeply about you. No, you aren't perfect. No one is. But you're loved, you're redeemed, you're a child of the King. So hold your head high and bask in His great love for you.

---

*Heavenly Father, guard me from defeatist thoughts.
Keep my focus on You and Your purpose for my life.
Let every day be a day of rejoicing in You.*

> *For bodily exercise profiteth little: but godliness is profitable unto all things, having promise of the life that now is, and of that which is to come.*
> —1 Timothy 4:8

NOVEMBER 28

Notice that the scripture says godliness is profitable unto all things. Godliness—being devout (fully committed) in faith—means treating others with dignity and respect, which improves personal relationships. Godliness builds a character of integrity, which benefits us in the home and the workplace. Godliness lets us set good examples for others to follow. Godliness shows the world that Jesus Christ makes a difference in a person's heart. We cannot go wrong when we choose to live a life of godliness.

Heavenly Father, let me be holy as You are holy. Set me apart for Your purpose, and may my works bring glory to Your name.

> *For this is good and acceptable in the sight of God our Saviour; Who will have all men to be saved, and to come unto the knowledge of the truth.*
> —1 Timothy 2:3-4

NOVEMBER 29

In so many ways, truth is in short supply these days. Telling the truth, the whole truth, and nothing but the truth is admirable and builds trust, but most people twist things to create their own version of "truth." But here is God's truth: all men are lost until they acknowledge their need for a Saviour and ask Jesus to save them. God desires that all men seek His Son. The Holy Spirit grows us in truth as we walk with Him. Knowledge of the Truth sets us free!

---

*Heavenly Father, salvation is available to any who choose to believe.
Please continue to call the lost.
Oh, Father, may none of Your precious creation reject the gift of Your Son.*

> Let the word of Christ dwell in you richly in all wisdom; teaching and admonishing one another in psalms and hymns and spiritual songs, singing with grace in your hearts to the Lord.
> —Colossians 3:16

NOVEMBER 30

"*...Dwell in you richly.*" I'm a fan of dark chocolate. The darker, the better, because the darker, the richer. Now that I've become accustomed to rich, dark chocolate, milk chocolate doesn't satisfy me anymore.

The same should be true for God's Word. The more we study and learn of Him, the less satisfying the things of the world become. The richness and fullness of His love and grace reaches deeper and deeper into our hearts until using foul talk or behaving in a hateful manner no longer rests easily on our conscience. The words of Christ have the power to change us for the better. And when we share His words with others, we have the chance to change their hearts for the better, too.

---

*Heavenly Father, whatever I say, whatever I do,
let it come from a heart dedicated to You
and let Your love flow through my words and actions.*

And the angel said unto them, Fear not: for, behold, I bring you good tidings of great joy, which shall be to all people.
—Luke 2:10

DECEMBER 1

I love the CHRISTmas season. I try so hard not to decorate my house before Thanksgiving (although I do listen to CHRISTmas music sometimes as early as July...), but the day after Thanksgiving, decorations explode! Some of my favorite pieces of decor are angels (probably because my dear Tante Lois, who now celebrates CHRISTmas in Heaven with Jesus, liked angels).

This simple statement—"I bring you good tidings of great joy"—should stir joy within our hearts. God made a promise to send a Savior. God kept that promise. Jesus Christ *is* our source of great joy! And He will be our focus the entire month of December. Celebrate with me!

(If you want to sing a CHRISTmas carol to go with today's message, I suggest "Angels, From the Realms of Glory" by James Montgomery.)

Heavenly Father, thank You for the great joy of Jesus! Thank You that He came for all.

And suddenly there was with the angel a multitude of the heavenly host praising God, and saying, Glory to God in the highest, and on earth peace, good will toward men.
—Luke 2:13-14

DECEMBER 2

Have you ever heard the saying, "There's strength in numbers"? It's true—lots of voices together make a bigger splash than a single voice. Can you imagine the shepherds' reaction when a great company of angels began praising God from the heavens? Can you imagine this hurting world's reaction if Christians everywhere began proclaiming Jesus's name openly and unashamedly? What a change might be wrought if we lost our worry about offending and simply began proclaiming the truth.

(Suggested carol: "Angels We Have Heard on High," a traditional French carol.)

---

*Heavenly Father, may I join with others
in proclaiming the truth of who You are.
Let our voices drown out deception and half truths.
May the world know that Jesus is King!*

> ...Where is he that is born King of the Jews? for we have seen his star in the east, and are come to worship him.
> —Matthew 2:2

DECEMBER 3

What a lengthy journey the three kings took to find the infant King. Years long, no doubt spending nights in uncomfortable places and sometimes going without a decent meal. Yet they weren't deterred. They wanted to find and worship the Baby.

Today people living in countries where Christianity is outlawed must journey through hardship to find and worship Jesus, but still they make the trek. Today people, whose families are part of strict religious groups that worship a different god, are banned from their parents' lives for choosing Jesus, and yet they choose Him. Are we willing to face hardship and rejection to worship the King?

(Suggested carol: "As With Gladness Men of Old" by William C. Dix.)

Heavenly Father, You promised to send the Messiah and You kept Your promise. Let me always bow down in worship to the one true King.

And she brought forth her firstborn son, and wrapped him in swaddling clothes, and laid him in a manger; because there was no room for them in the inn.
—Luke 2:7

DECEMBER 4

I'm a pretty imaginative person, but I have a hard time envisioning what Mary must have felt as she gave birth in a lowly animal stall and placed her precious baby boy in a feeding trough. Mary knew who He was—the angel had told her. Even if she hadn't known, every mother's heart wants the very best for her child. Mary had to have longed for a warm room, a beautiful cradle lined with soft linen, the delicate essence of incense rather than the odor of beasts and straw welcoming her child into the world. Her heart must have ached to see her firstborn son given such a humble beginning. Yet this was God's plan for His Son—a humble beginning, a Savior not just for the rich or powerful but for every man. For me. For you. For all of mankind.

(Suggested carol: "Gentle Mary Laid Her Child" by Joseph Simpson Cook.)

*Heavenly Father, You sent Your Son for me.
Thank You for the incredible gift of salvation.*

Of this man's seed hath God according to his promise raised unto Israel a Saviour, Jesus:
—Acts 13:23

DECEMBER 5

"*...According to his promise...*" Those are such incredible, powerful words. When God makes a promise, He keeps it. He promised Israel they could expect a Savior. He paved the way for Christ's birth, and when the time was ripe, He sent His very own precious, perfect, sinless Son into this world. Not a king in royal garb, not a soldier armed for battle, but a Baby, a child who would grow and laugh and love and experience hardship and temptations and hurt feelings like any other human. In this way, He could relate to all of us. He could give an example to all of us.

Yes, God sent His Promise: Jesus Christ.

(Suggested carol: "Carols Sing" by Paul E. Puckett.)

Heavenly Father, thank You for keeping Your promises. I know I can depend on You.

And without controversy great is the mystery of godliness: God was manifest in the flesh, justified in the Spirit, seen of angels, preached unto the Gentiles, believed on in the world, received up into glory.
—1 Timothy 3:16

DECEMBER 6

In this single verse is the entirety of Christ's life. God in the flesh walking our earth to become the sin sacrifice for all mankind. Because I believe in Him, on the day I leave my earthly body, I will be with Him in Glory. That statement gives me all the hope and security I need to navigate life's pathway.

Salvation is no mystery, it's simply a matter of trusting that He is who says He is.

(Suggested carol: "Christmas Has Its Cradle" by Rae E. Whitney.)

Heavenly Father, You unraveled the mysteries of sin and death and provided a Solution: Jesus Christ. Thank You that I am saved and secure!

And we declare unto you glad tidings, how that the promise which was made unto the fathers, God hath fulfilled the same unto us their children, in that he hath raised up Jesus again; as it is also written in the second psalm, Thou art my Son, this day have I begotten thee.
—Acts 13:32-33

DECEMBER 7

There are so many people in this world who don't have an earthly father or who have fathers who aren't the kind of man God intended to lead families. When a child's father disappoints or abandons him, it can be hard for him to feel secure. He may even be bitter or resentful. It can also make it hard for that child to see God as loving, kind, and available. But God is a father who will never abandon us, never discourage us, never mislead us.

We become God's child by accepting Jesus as our Savior. Once His, we have all the security, hope, peace, and joy we need. Beautiful statement of promise, "...I have begotten thee." Child of God, remember how much you are loved.

(Suggested carol: "Child in the Manger" by Mary MacDonald.)

Heavenly Father, thank You for being a Father who loves and cares unendingly for His children. Thank You for being my Father.

> *Behold, a virgin shall be with child, and shall bring forth a son, and they shall call his name Emmanuel, which being interpreted is, God with us.*
> —Matthew 1:23

DECEMBER 8

God with us. Read that again: God with us. Not God far away above the clouds and inaccessible. Not God in a castle lording over us. Not God turning His back on us stumbling, needy, inept sheep. But God *with* us.

Jesus came. He wore human skin and experienced human emotions and pain. Because of His choice to live among us, He knows exactly how we feel in every life circumstance. Which means He is able to communicate our needs, our pains, our joys, our sorrows, our thoughts, our fears, our...everything...to the Father. Then the Spirit came. He indwells us. He guides and directs and encourages us.

God with us. With *us*. We are never alone.

(Suggested carol: "O Come, O Come, Emmanuel" by John Mason Neale.)

Heavenly Father, I don't know why You want to be with me, but thank You. I am never alone because of You.

The next day John seeth Jesus coming unto him, and saith, Behold the Lamb of God, which taketh away the sin of the world.
—John 1:29

DECEMBER 9

For centuries, people had anticipated their coming Messiah. If you were standing in the crowd the day John the Baptist pointed to Jesus and made the claim in John 1:29, would you have been surprised, elated, or disappointed by Jesus' appearance? After all, the people expected a mighty warrior who would rescue them from their oppressors. What they didn't know is God had sent a humble Lamb to rescue them from themselves. Sin is ugly. It harms, it divides, it destroys. It promises death. But Jesus brings us *life*.

Look! The Lamb of God has come! And He's coming again.

(Suggested carol: "Come, Thou Long-Expected Jesus" by Charles Wesley.)

Heavenly Father, thank You for sending Your Son into this needy, hurting world. You knew what we wanted, yet You sent what we needed: a Savior. Thank You that He will come again and take me to be with You.

And when they had seen it, they made known abroad the saying which was told them concerning this child.
—Luke 2:17

DECEMBER 10

Do you remember the day you accepted Jesus as Savior and Lord? I was only eight years old, but I can still recall the wonder that all my sins were gone and that now I was a Christian. The first thing I did was find my mom and dad (because I made the decision at the close of Sunday school) and tell them. I wanted them to know.

That's the way it is when we meet Jesus—we want others to know. We want to proclaim what He's done for us. He saved me! Healed me! Strengthened me! Comforted me! I want to proclaim it, and God wants me to proclaim it because those who've not yet believed need to hear. Spread the Word, Christian—shout it from the rooftops: Jesus Christ is Lord!

(Suggested carol: "Go, Tell It on the Mountain" by John W. Work, Jr.)

Heavenly Father, thank You for sending my sins far away. May my life display my gratitude in what I say and do.

Glory to God in the highest, and on earth peace, good will toward men.
—Luke 2:14

DECEMBER 11

God sent Jesus to bring us peace. When we think of peace, we often think it means a lack of conflict. Jesus' peace is ours *in spite of* conflict.

This world, because of its sin nature, will always have conflict. But we can experience peace when we rest in the knowledge of His love for us. We can bring moments of peace to others by performing deeds of good will. Hopefully our lives will pierce the dark cloud of sin and hurt with the light of God's love.

(Suggested carol: "Hark! The Herald Angels Sing" by Charles Wesley.)

Heavenly Father, You do bring peace.
I've experienced it in the midst of life's storms.
Thank You for giving what the world cannot: peace.

Therefore with joy shall ye draw water out of the wells of salvation.
—Isaiah 12:3

DECEMBER 12

Isaiah foretold the promise of the coming Savior, the One who would bring salvation to the Jews and also to the Gentiles. Notice the verse says "with joy." There is joy in knowing our sins are forgiven. There is joy in knowing we are loved by the Almighty King. There is joy in knowing a mansion is ready for us in Heaven. Joy! Joy! Joy! Joy is the word for the season, and for those of us who stand unashamed and spotless before God, joy should be a part of our daily lives.

(Suggested carol: "How Great Our Joy," a traditional German carol.)

Heavenly Father, help me remember happiness is fleeting but joy is eternal.
Thank You for the joy You bestow on Your children.

> *But thou, Bethlehem Ephratah, though thou be little among the thousands of Judah, yet out of thee shall he come forth unto me that is to be ruler in Israel; whose goings forth have been from of old, from everlasting. And this man shall be the peace...*
> —Micah 5:2, 5a

DECEMBER 13

In the beginning was the Word, and the Word was with God, and the Word was God. The Word is Jesus. From the beginning He was there. From the beginning He knew His purpose. Being God, He could have chosen to avoid the pain of crucifixion, but being one with God, He understood the consequences for mankind if He refused the road to Calvary. He was a Ruler yet a Servant; a King yet humble. He bears many names, and one of them is Prince of Peace. He is our source of peace.

(Suggested carol: "I Heard the Bells on Christmas Day" by Henry W. Longfellow.)

Heavenly Father, thank You for loving me enough to make a plan for me to have peace in my heart. Thank You for Jesus, the Prince of Peace.

And the angel said unto them, Fear not: for, behold, I bring you good tidings of great joy, which shall be to all people.
—Luke 2:10

DECEMBER 14

My cats don't like thunder and lightning. A host of angels would be even more startling. And not only to cats! So of course the angel's first order of business was to assure the shepherds they needn't be afraid. Then wonderful words followed: Great joy, the promised Messiah, had come for *all* people. Even the lowly, the outcast, the stinky smelly ostracized shepherds.

God spoke volumes by sending the angel to the lowliest of the lowly. Many people think they need to straighten up or change their ways and *then* seek God. Nope, not necessary. God loves us where we are. Loves us enough to send His Son to us. "Good tidings of great joy"–in a word, Jesus.

(Suggested carol: "Angels From the Realms of Glory" by James Montgomery.)

Heavenly Father, Your unconditional love and acceptance humbles me. May I love others the way You love– without prejudice or stipulations.

For God so loved the world, that he gave his only begotten Son, that whosoever believeth in him should not perish, but have everlasting life.
—John 3:16

DECEMBER 15

You see a lot of evergreens around CHRISTmastime. Evergreens always remind me of eternal life, and the thought of eternal life always brings to mind this very familiar verse. God's gift of Jesus was beyond priceless. His precious Son, sent to be our sin sacrifice, entered this world so that God could enjoy a relationship with us. His love for us is beyond measure. All He wants is our belief and trust... and eternity with Him is ours. The wonders of His love!

(Suggested carol: "Joy to the World! The Lord is Come" by Isaac Watts.)

Heavenly Father, there aren't words enough to express my gratitude for salvation, which frees me from sin's curse. May my life show my gratitude.

> *Sing unto the Lord,*
> *O ye saints of his,*
> *and give thanks at*
> *the remembrance*
> *of his holiness.*
> —Psalm 30:4

DECEMBER 16

Word of the Father appeared in flesh in the form of a tiny, helpless, humble baby. Often artists paint a halo around the infant Jesus in the manger, a reference to His holiness.

Did you know that you, as a believer, are also holy? The Bible calls us to holiness—being consecrated to God's service and conforming our lives to the will of God, just as Christ did. Being holy is a "work in progress," and we will face many challenges. But when we remember Christ's example and strive to follow it, we will achieve holiness.

(Suggested carol: "O Come, All Ye Faithful" by John Francis Wade.)

Heavenly Father, being holy in an unholy world is hard.
Thank You for Your Spirit who strengthens and emboldens me.

And she brought forth her firstborn son, and wrapped him in swaddling clothes, and laid him in a manger; because there was no room for them in the inn.
—Luke 2:7

DECEMBER 17

December 17th in the mid-1980's, I became mommy for the second time. My baby arrived earlier than her anticipated date, but I'd prepared a room with a cradle, little sleepers, and all the other things I needed for my new baby. Mary gave birth far from her home. She had no diapers or little gowns or a cradle in which to place her newborn son. But the Bible doesn't mention her worrying or even complaining. Instead, she pondered the event.

There wasn't room for Jesus in the inn, but there was room in the hearts of all who witnessed this birth. Is there room in your heart for the Christ child?

(Suggested carol: "Infant Holy, Infant Lowly," a Polish carol paraphrased by Edith M. G. Reed.)

Heavenly Father, open my heart wide to receive Your Son as my Redeemer and Savior, and let Him be the Lord of my life.

And Joseph also went up from Galilee, out of the city of Nazareth, into Judaea, unto the city of David, which is called Bethlehem; (because he was of the house and lineage of David:)
—Luke 2:4

DECEMBER 18

Maybe because I'm a woman who's given birth, this scripture leads me to Mary. At that stage of her pregnancy, straddling a donkey and riding so many miles had to have been miserable. The Bible tells us that Mary was a devout girl, so she must have known the prophecies surrounding the One who would save the Jewish people. She must have known the importance of Bethlehem. But did she fully understand that she *carried* the promised Messiah? We don't know. But she traveled to Bethlehem in obedience to her husband and to Caesar Augustus's decree. And prophecy was fulfilled.

When we don't understand, when it means being uncomfortable, will we still be obedient and go where He leads?

(Suggested carol: "O Little Town of Bethlehem" by Phillips Brooks)

Heavenly Father, may I obey Your promptings
and trust You even when the way isn't clear.
Thank You for always guiding me to a place of blessing.

> *But Jesus called them unto him, and said, Suffer little children to come unto me, and forbid them not: for of such is the kingdom of God.*
> —Luke 18:16

DECEMBER 19

Jesus, although weary and overwhelmed, chastised His disciples when they tried to hold back the children from "bothering" Him. In Matthew 18, He says unless people become like little children, they cannot enter the kingdom of Heaven.

You see, children innately trust. If Daddy holds out his arms and says, "Jump," a child will do so without a moment's pause. This is the kind of trust Jesus wants from us—to take Him at His word that He is our Messiah. To trust that He will be with us every step of life's journey. To trust that we will reside with Him eternally when our time on earth is done. Jesus wants nothing more than for us to take a leap of faith into His outstretched arms.

(Suggested carol "Oh, Come, Little Children" by Johann P. Schultz.)

Heavenly Father, You are trustworthy.
If I am holding anything back from You,
give me the courage let go and let You work Your will in me.

> ...Christ Jesus: Who, being in the form of God, thought it not robbery to be equal with God: But made himself of no reputation, and took upon him the form of a servant, and was made in the likeness of men:
> —Philippians 2:5a-7

DECEMBER 20

Jesus was fully God and yet fully man. The wonder of God's inner workings are sometimes too lofty for us to understand. And that's okay. God doesn't expect us to *understand* His ways; He expects us to trust His ways.

Jesus, the Son of God, took on the form of a servant. All the powers of heaven were in His hands, but He didn't use His power to serve Himself. Instead, He performed miracles that benefited mankind and pointed to His Father. As His followers, we're expected to serve, but not to bring attention and accolades on ourselves. We want to bring attention to the One who created us, redeemed us, and resides within us.

(Suggested carol: "Thou Didst Leave Thy Throne" by Emily E.S. Elliott.)

---

*Heavenly Father, Your ways are beyond the scope
of my comprehension,
and at the same time I know that You are here with me.
Let my trust in You continue to grow.*

And there shall come forth a rod out of the stem of Jesse, and a Branch shall grow out of his roots: And the spirit of the LORD shall rest upon him, the spirit of wisdom and understanding, the spirit of counsel and might, the spirit of knowledge and of the fear of the LORD...
—Isaiah 11:1-2

DECEMBER 21

Jesus is coming again. He is coming to judge the earth with discernment and truth—no one will fool Him with glibly stated falsehoods. Those who oppose Him and those who perform wicked deeds will be brought low. And on that day, the wolf and the lamb will lie together in peace. What a glorious time that will be...for the redeemed. Those of us who are saved need not fear the coming of the Lord. It's an event to be anticipated. Not so for those who work against Him or who have rejected Him, though.

The time is drawing nigh. His return is closer every day. Are we ready to meet Jesus?

(Suggested carol: "Lo, How a Rose E'er Blooming" by Theodore Baker.)

---

*Heavenly Father, You promised Jesus will return,
and You keep Your promises.
Ready my heart for His coming
and let me share Him so none will be left behind.*

And, lo, the angel of the Lord came upon them, and the glory of the Lord shone round about them: and they were sore afraid.
—Luke 2:9

DECEMBER 22

I was healed from six chronic illnesses in one fell swoop on September 20, 2004. I'd left for a conference relying on a cane; the day after my return, I ran to meet my husband's truck when he came home from work. His response: "You're running. This is creeping me out." My overnight change frightened him; he couldn't comprehend how it happened. Any surprising change can bring confusion and fear.

The shepherds reacted to the angels' sudden appearance with fright. But when God's behind the event, there's no need to be afraid. Sure, getting a blast of the glory of the Lord is startling, but as the angels said, fear not. Everything He sends us is for our good.

(Suggested carol: "Break Forth, O Beauteous Heavenly Light" by Johann von Rist.)

Heavenly Father, I might not understand what I encounter, but I trust the goodness of Your heart and know You are working in my best interest.

> *Make a joyful noise unto the Lord,*
> *all the earth: make a loud noise,*
> *and rejoice, and sing praise.*
> —Psalm 98:4

DECEMBER 23

This verse encapsulates the heart of worship—make a joyful noise unto the Lord. Even nature sings His praise. Have you heard the music in the rush of a waterfall, the whisper of wind, the call of geese tracing a path against the evening sky? The silence of a glacier is a song unto itself.

We praise the Lord for who He is. Because He came. Because He's coming again. Because nothing and no one can separate us from the love of God. So raise a song of praise. The decibels or even the purity of tone don't matter. He hears the heart, and that makes our praise a sweet melody in His ears.

(Suggested carol: "Joy to the World! The Lord is Come!" by Isaac Watts.)

Heavenly Father, let my life be a song of praise
to You, my Lord and Redeemer.

> *And when they were come into the house, they saw the young child with Mary his mother, and fell down, and worshipped him: and when they had opened their treasures, they presented unto him gifts; gold, and frankincense and myrrh.*
> —Matthew 2:11

DECEMBER 24

Gold, frankincense, and myrrh. Such unlikely gifts for a new child. But this wasn't an ordinary child—this child was the King of kings. These gifts symbolized who Jesus was. Each gift carried a significance His parents might have pondered as they struggled with the knowledge of Who they were raising as their own.

Gold—a fitting gift for someone of royal birth; frankincense—an incense used in ceremonial worship of the deity; myrrh—an oil used to prepare bodies for burial. These gifts gave hints to Jesus' life, ministry, and eventual sacrifice. The kings brought costly, valuable gifts as part of their worship. What of value will I lay at Jesus' feet in my worship of Him?

(Suggested carol: "Sing We Now of Christmas," translated into English from the French carol, "Noël Nouvelet.")

Heavenly Father, Your Son is worthy of my worship and praise. May I always bring Him my best.

For unto you is born this day in the city of David a Saviour, which is Christ the Lord.
—Luke 2:11

DECEMBER 25

Merry CHRISTmas! In most households, there are brightly wrapped gifts waiting to be opened. I once saw a short video of a child tossing aside a gift because he didn't like the bow on the box. Some toss Jesus aside because they don't like the idea of bowing to Him in submission, and look what they miss: freedom from sin's penalties; a Shepherd who guides and protects; a source of peace, comfort, and strength. Oh, what a precious gift came for all! But not all will receive Him.

On this CHRISTmas day, let's pray for the lost to come to a place of recognition for their need of a Savior. What better gift to God than welcoming new believers into His family.

(Suggested carol: "Silent Night, Holy Night" by Joseph Mohr. For the story behind this beloved carol, visit home.snu.edu/~hculbert/silent.htm.)

---

*Heavenly Father, thank You for sending Jesus to earth.
May this CHRISTmas day be a day of new birth
for someone I love.*

Thine eyes did see my substance, yet being unperfect; and in thy book all my members were written, which in continuance were fashioned, when as yet there was none of them.
—Psalm 139:16

DECEMBER 26

From the beginning of time, God had a plan for His Son, Jesus, to enter this earth, walk among us, then serve as a sacrifice for our sins and be a mediator between man and God. It was a glorious plan, one beyond our comprehension, yet made with tremendous love and compassion. That very same God, from the beginning of time, knew there would be a *you*. He longed for fellowship with you, and made great plans for you—plans He knew would bring you joy and fulfillment. How much you are loved…

*Heavenly Father, thank You for loving me.
Let me never forget how much I mean to You.*

Through the tender mercy of our God; whereby the dayspring from on high hath visited us...
—Luke 1:78

DECEMBER 27

*G*od loves *us*. God hates *sin*. He knows that when we are trapped in sin we cannot be happy with ourselves or with anyone else. So He provided a way to freedom: the Dawn that brings light to the dark souls of men...our Savior, Jesus Christ. His merciful compassion goes beyond anything our feeble minds can comprehend, but when we accept it, our lives change.

*Heavenly Father, You have brought a change to my heart.
Thank You for the joy of walking in the Light.*

> *In my distress I cried unto the LORD, and he heard me.*
> —Psalm 120:1

DECEMBER 28

I love my husband. I really do. He's a man of many talents and he uses them to serve others. He's just not always a very good listener because his mind is usually flipping through lots of files instead of focusing on the one I'm holding open. I guess you could say he's human.

But you know what? There is One who is never too busy to hear me. When I need a listening ear, He is available. He keys in on every word I utter (and even hears and understands my wordless groanings), and He responds to comfort me, guide me, strengthen me. I am so grateful the LORD is there...24-7!

Need a Listener? Call out. He's there.

Heavenly Father, You are a God who never slumbers.
Whenever I need You, You're here.
Thank You for being so attentive to me.

> *He hath made his wonderful works to be remembered: the LORD is gracious and full of compassion.*
> —Psalm 111:4

DECEMBER 29

*E*ven as a kid, I loved cloud-watching, star-watching, moon-watching, sunbeam-watching... My parents finally had to adjust to my random gasps from the back seat of the car when a unique cloud or fingers of sunlight or a bright star caught my attention.

When I admire the wonder of the sky, I can't help but also consider the Creator. Such beauty He built into this world! Such tender care He bestows on His children. Every star, sunbeam, and fluffy cloud is a physical reminder of the One who holds me in His hands.

Rest in His gracious compassion today, remember the wonderful works He has performed in your life, and praise Him for all He has done.

---

*Heavenly Father, thank You for the beauty of the sky
that speaks of Your presence.
Thank You for not only holding the stars
but holding this child.*

O praise the Lord, all ye nations: praise him, all ye people.
For his merciful kindness is great toward us:
and the truth of the Lord endureth for ever.
Praise ye the Lord.
—Psalm 117

DECEMBER 30

Can you measure the volume of the oceans? Can you see the end of the horizon? Both are impossible. I cannot fathom the scope of this world and the breadth and depth of those mighty bodies of water. And just as immeasurable as the ocean's contents and the horizon's reach is God's love for us. His love and faithfulness endure *forever*. His love and faithfulness are without measure and without end. Praise and glory be to God for His wonderful gifts!

Heavenly Father, there is nothing besides You
that is forever. I praise You for always being here for me.

*My soul, wait thou only
upon God;
For my expectation
[hope] is from him.*
—Psalm 62:5

DECEMBER 31

I don't suppose it's any secret my favorite word is "hope." People without hope are, in my humble opinion, the saddest people in the world. Christians, however, are *never* without hope, because we know Jesus already has the victory The Bible says so, and God's Word does not lie. We know we are loved—Jesus proved it on Calvary. We know we have a home waiting in heaven—Jesus promised it. Nothing of this world can change any of those truths. So we can cling to His promises and remember that circumstances never change who we are to Him and who He is to us.

As the psalmist said, my hope is in *Him*!

---

*Heavenly Father, You truly are my Hope and Stay.
Let me put my full trust in Your guidance,
and may my every step bring glory to You.*

Est. 2013

Wings of Hope Publishing is committed to providing quality Christian reading material in both the fiction and non-fiction markets.

Made in the USA
Monee, IL
09 November 2023